The Art and Science of Motor Cycle Road Racing

The Art
and Science of
Motor Cycle
Road Racing

Peter Clifford

Hazleton Publishing, Richmond, Surrey

This second edition published in 1985 by Hazleton Publishing,
3 Richmond Hill, Richmond, Surrey TW10 6RE

ISBN 0 905138 35 X

Printed in Holland by drukkerij de Lange/van Leer b.v., Deventer
Typesetting by C. Leggett & Son Ltd., Mitcham, Surrey, England

Cover photographs by Chief Photographer, Don Morley
Colour photography by:
Don Morley – pages 17, 18, 35, 36, 117, 118, 135, 169, 187, 188, 237, 238, 255, 256
Peter Clifford – pages 136, 170

Black and white photography by:
Don Morley
Hazel Coad
Peter Clifford
Ray Daniels
Jim Greening
Shigeo Kibiki
Lou Martin
Gerry Stream

The Author acknowledges with thanks the valued assistance of:
Harald Bartol, Alain Chevallier, Ciba Geigy, Dunlop Limited,
Anne-Marie Gerber (FIM), Henk Keulemans, Dennis Noyce, Paolo
Scalera, Gunther Weisinger, Ron Williams

All those riders who answered unlimited questions and without whose
help this book could never have been written

All circuit officers who provided information for Chapter 7.

Contents

Foreword: Kenny Roberts

I'm sure that motor cycle racing is one hundred per cent science. For me art is something that you just do: there it is, you've done it and you needn't know how. If that was the case with motor cycle racing I wouldn't have to spend days before a race testing, practising. I could just fly in, race the bike and go home.

No, it's a science. It's the relationship between power, gyro effects, engine torque, G forces, all the things that make the bike go a little bit quicker around the track. You have to be able to use every little piece of momentum. If you could programme a computer to know all the things that you know after years of racing, then it could do the thing for you.

I might spend one and a half hours laying in the truck, thinking about a couple of places on the track where I'm having trouble. I think about it and run through it in my mind, just as I ride it. What I see and feel comes back to me: the feel of the suspension, steering and brakes. I play it back time and time again until I isolate what I think the problem is. It might be a double left hander, followed by a right. I'm going into the first left too fast, on the brakes and then accelerating through the second. That's putting me out of the second left fast with the power on but because the power is on I have to have the bike more upright and I can't get back across to the left for the next right which is real close.

I decide that I've got to keep my momentum up more through the corner, not brake so hard for the second left, run through it smooth and fast without so much acceleration so I can keep it leaned over hard bringing myself back over to the left in good shape to flick the bike in for the right.

Once I've worked out the answer to the problem, it's fixed in my mind so that next time I go out on the track I will just do it. I won't be thinking about it, it should be dialled in.

When you can think about riding a motor cycle, understand what it is doing and know how to improve it, then you don't have to go getting yourself pumped up to ride it fast. I can still get pumped up but it isn't necessary for a good performance. If you comprehend what the bike is doing then you'll know its limits and be able to ride it to its maximum without wondering whether you're going to fall off any second.

You can teach guys to race, or rather what you really do is save them time. If they're any good they'd find out sooner or later anyway. What you can do is to watch them, ask them questions about why they do certain things and give them plenty to think about. By the time a guy's got to riding in Grands Prix there's probably not too much that you can teach him. On the other hand I could still do with somebody watching me who I could trust who really

understood what the motor cycle was doing because even feelings are hard to pin point sometimes and it would be useful to have a well-trained observer or a high speed movie camera on some occasions.

What this book is about is understanding why the motor cycle does what it does, how the physical laws affect the motion of the machine and what the rider does about making the best of them. If you're going to be a good road racer then you've got to learn to do the same because whoever you are and whatever you're riding you've got what you've got and you've got to learn to make the best of it. It's no good standing there complaining that the tyres are no good, the bike doesn't handle or that the works bikes are so fast that you haven't got a chance. The works riders have got where they are because they've taken machines that are less and made them more. The purpose is to put in one hundred and ten per cent effort and that's the only way you'll succeed.

Introduction

This is the second edition of a book that had to be out of date the day after it was written but for the most part will be as true in ten or twenty years as it was when it was originally written. Machines, riders and circuits change and a completely new chapter called "New Technology" covers the latest advances but the basic principles of riding and the laws of physics do not alter and certainly artistry does not date. So while it was not possible to change every reference to machines and riders the second edition I hope will be enjoyed as much as the first which was sold out making the reprinting and revision necessary.

While researching for this book I found in an old and treasured volume a reference to the Isle of Man TT regulations from the early years of the competition. A section of the regulations under the heading 'Requirements' was quoted: 'Material: The machine shall comprise a frame, two wheels and a suitable engine'.

I am sure that it was ever so, and shall remain so until man no longer desires to race motor cycles. The disarming simplicity of the stated requirement underlines the very nature of motor cycle racing even today. The motor cycles remain essentially simple machines, the beauty of the sport being that complexity brings increased weight and size and both are the enemies of speed.

In broad terms the motor cycle still looks very similar to the machines raced in the early days of the sport. Even when considered in detail some facets of design have been simplified while others have become more complex. Modern disc and power valve engines may seem complicated but not if compared with the four stroke multi cylinder engines of the past. Suspension systems are quite often blessed with an arrangement of connecting rods and levers unknown ten years ago but in the same time wire wheels with separate rims and hubs have largely been replaced by single cast units.

Although machines may not have become vastly more complex the technology involved in their production has progressed tremendously and specialist knowledge of materials science, electronics, welding techniques, aerodynamics' etc. has become vital for engineers and designers. The constraints imposed by the desire to minimise the machines' size and weight have been put under tremendous pressure by engine developments which produce more and more power and advances in tyre design which allow that power to be transmitted to the ground and the machines to travel ever faster round the corners. This book attempts to explain the conflicts that must be overcome in designing a racing machine.

Far from laying out hard lines which control the design of every racing motor cycle, I have tried to illustrate some of the widely differing opinions held by equally well respected engineers. Racing engineering is an exact science, but only when the particular problem and its solution can be isolated and studied. Very often limitations on time and money make isolation impossible, one effect masks another and intuition must take over from calculation. Science gives way to art.

And what of the men who use these advanced pieces of machinery, who guide and force them around the racing circuits of the world? How do they make their motor cycle perform better, and circulate faster than the next man? There are physical laws that govern the performance of men and machine. The rider must use one physical principle against another so that the net result is the machine going where he wants it to at the required speed.

The rider may, or may not, understand exactly what he is doing. He may act out of instinct or it may be a calculated operation. Calculation or instinct, art or science?

When you watch a machine sweeping through a curve it can seem pure magic, but if you prefer not to believe in wizardry this book will explain the forces at work and give some idea of the skill required to balance the equations. If you like the mystique of the secret racing engine and the gravity defying antics of each world champion don't be afraid to read on because understanding all that is inside will only lead you to ask more searching questions.

Peter Clifford.

13

1

The rider

"If I were not a motor cycle road racer", said Franco Uncini, "I would like to be an astronaut and fly the space shuttle Columbia. I suppose I'm a fighter; I don't like things to come easily and I love racing." Franco's view point is typical of many riders. They thrive on competition and almost certainly on the danger that is a calculated risk, and that is why it is not unusual to find that riders have switched to racing from riding motor cycles on the road.

Richard Schlachter's experience sums that up: "My first bike was a Mota Beta 100. The second day I had it I took it down to the local gravel pit to do some dirt riding. When it was time to come home I came flying down the dirt road from the pit, around a blind corner, and smack into the front of an on-coming car. I went over the handlebars and took some soil samples with my face and though I wasn't hurt much, the bike was a wreck. The front wheel was bent up underneath the engine and I was so mad I just dragged it home. A year or so later I sold the Beta and bought a 500 Kawasaki. That was necessary as most of my mates had Kawas and I was having a hard time keeping up. We all went down to Daytona and that was my first look at big-time road racing. I gaped at all the works teams' transporters, the factory bikes and all the speed and excitement. I thought just how fantastic it would be to be part of it but it never occurred to me that I could do any racing.

"Of course, my mates and I talked about it a lot and then when we were back home in Old Lyme one of the guys heard over the radio that the local club was running a road race at Bridgehampton, Long Island. Anyone could go and race – just put number plates on and wire up your drain plugs. He told it to me like a bit of a dare so we rushed down to the spares shop and I bought a pair of leather motocross jeans to go with my road riding jacket. We fixed the numbers and the drain plugs and turned up to race at Bridgehampton. On the sixth lap the bike seized. I'd no idea about jetting and, anyway, how do you read a surface gap plug? But by then I was hooked. The track was so neat, it's still one of my favourites. You can charge round flat out; there were no cars

coming the other way, no dogs running out, no cops.

"One of the guys who went with us was Dave Roper. When we found that there was a four hour endurance race a couple of days later, Dave and I decided to ride. It had already sunk in that his Big Horn Kawasaki wasn't a very good dirt bike so we took the front forks, wheel and all, off my Kawasaki and put it on his 350 single. We didn't have entries for the race so we talked our way in: 'Yeah, sure we're here to race. We're the pros from Old Lyme'. I'd talked my way into any job I had ever had so I'd got plenty of practice at convincing people that I knew what I was doing. Practice went great, we were having a ball. As it was three quarters his bike, Dave started the race first but on lap two it seized going downhill at a hundred miles an hour and pitched him into the ground. He was bruised all over but he loved it. The racing bug had bit hard."

"Of course, I never got to ride the Big Horn. When I put the forks back on my Kawasaki, every penny I earned went into buying bits for it. I got a Fontana front brake and in those days that was the real thing. Trick pipes, and I rode it at club races all across the East Coast. It was one long round of parties and barbecues, the racing

Richard Schlachter, on the 500 Kawasaki that he raced around the Club circuits of North America's East Coast. So many road racers start this way riding modified production machines in un-named leathers.

was great and so was the social life. We'd get drunk on Saturday night and then go out and race like hell on Sunday. But even then I cared about winning and the pressure I put on myself then is the same pressure I feel now to beat the other guy. Its the same whether he's Dave Roper from down the street or Toni Mang from West Germany."

So Richard Schlachter fell in love with motor cycle road racing and surely all riders would have to love racing because it does not seem logical to balance the effort and danger involved merely against the monetary rewards that can be obtained. But liking something and wanting to be successful at it cannot be enough to make a world championship class rider. To win you must be in some way better than the other man. Randy Mamola cites determination as the major factor: "I wasn't just born a good rider. You've got to have determination if you are to get better and better. When I was a kid I was determined to be a great drummer; I thought Ringo Starr and the Beatles were it and that was what I wanted to do. I did get good at it – I'd been practising since I was eight – and I think that also helped me develop my sense of co-ordination. When I signed to ride dirt track for Yamaha they wanted me to play the drums as well. It made good publicity to have me doing both.

"What dirt track racing taught me more than anything was to beat the fear of speed. Even on the small bikes I was racing then you went fast and real close on tight tracks. When I first tried road racing it seemed real easy. The thing I had to learn to do then was ride smoothly and my Dad would always say to me just before I'd go out to race 'Ride smooth, son, ride smooth'. He still does. When I was dirt tracking I just used to go out and nail it. It was close and physical. Now with road racing, smooth is the key."

Randy Mamola learned to ride a motor cycle fast on the dirt, applied what he knew to road racing and made adjustments where necessary. But is becoming a brilliant road racer all in learning, and how vital is natural talent? Are World Champions born or are they made? That, says Kork Ballington, is a very interesting question.

"I think you have to be born with the basic ingredients: a sense of balance and co-ordination. These can be developed but you have to have something there to start with. The less suited you are to be a road racer, the harder work it will be. I'm lucky, I've never felt I had to try very hard to ride fast; it seemed to come easy to me right from the start and as I progressed my riding just developed naturally."

There can be few people who would suggest that Kenny Roberts is anything but full of natural talent but he actually puts the accent

Kork Ballington on the 500cc Kawasaki leads Marc Fontan at Jarama.

Kenny Roberts on his 500cc Yamaha at Daytona.

on the thinking effort necessary to go fast because no matter how great your talent for riding a motor cycle fast if someone else is better at setting up the machine's suspension or correcting its steering geometry, then their motor cycle will be so much better that it will be easy to ride it quickly. As far as Kenny is concerned his dirt track racing taught him how to ride a motor cycle fast and that gave him a head start when he got on a road racer. He had racing talent as well but even those two factors couldn't take him to the top and he began to learn from those around him. At that time it was Kel Carruthers the Australian who went to America with a wealth of Grand Prix racing experience. He led the road racing team that Kenny joined and for a while at least Kenny followed him on the track.

Kel recalls those days when they both raced Yamaha twins, painted yellow and black: "Part of my job as manager/rider for the American Yamaha road race team was to pass on what I could of my racing knowledge to Kenny Roberts. He'd got plenty of talent and was already pretty good. In fact he won his first road race and thought it was real easy. Then I think he fell off three times in his second race and realised that it wasn't quite that simple. What we'd do was go out to practice together, rather than me run away and hide, practising on my own. I tried to impress on Kenny the importance of going fast through fast corners. I'd learned to really like fast circuits in Europe, especially real road circuits like the Isle of Man TT course, Spa and Czechoslovakia.

"When I came to the States I found that most of the tracks had slow corners but I knew that if Kenny ever went to Europe he needed to know how to go through fast bends. If you go through a fast corner right, you'll make up time. Try hard through slow corners and you'll never make up anything. Any really good rider will be fast round quick corners and the risks of falling off on slow bends are much too high for it to be worth while.

And there was Cal Rayborn, the brilliant number one rider for Harley-Davidson. "I already had the ability to be able to keep up with Kel, but he had a fantastic amount of experience. When we went to tracks that were really fast or particularly difficult I could learn a lot from him. I also used to watch Cal and the two of them had very different styles. Kel used a lot of front engine weight which made the front wheel do all the steering. Cal had the engine and the centre of gravity further back and used to steer more with the back wheel, getting the power on early in the corners.

"But those two guys both had neat, tucked in riding styles. Though I didn't realise it at the time that was holding me back. I was then a big fan of Jarno Saarinen. He was obviously fast: he'd

won the 250 World Championship and his style was amazing. I only saw him race once and that was when he came to Ontario and even that was just for a few laps because he fell off and broke his shoulder but it really set me thinking. It struck me that it might be the way to enable the back end to drift and still feel comfortable.

"Kel and I went there the year after. There was one horseshoe where I was not comfortable. One lap I decided to lean off like Paul Smart was doing and it worked, it felt a lot faster. In the second heat I just split away from Kel, using the hanging off to make me feel more comfortable going faster. The next race was Daytona the following March. I was sore then from an accident and couldn't

move about on the bike but then we went to Dallas and I started dragging my knee on the ground through the turns. I had to put super tape on my knees and everyone cracked up. Kel said: 'Jesus, what the hell are we going to have next?'

Early days for Barry Sheene on his Bultaco.

"After that, and especially when I went to England, I started to think not only about my riding but about the race as well. There's not much practice time at English meetings so if you want to learn to go fast you've got to fill in by re-running the track in your mind while you sit in the truck. In fact, when I'm on the bike I don't think consciously about the bike or the track I just do it by feel. I shift gear with feel, knowing what the engine is doing. Sometimes at the end of a straight, or occasionally at the beginning I look at the rev counter to see what it is doing but I never look at the water temperature gauge unless the mechanics ask me to do so specifically and then they'll probably have to ask me six times."

Kenny Roberts certainly seems like the archetypal computer brain while Barry Sheene, who prides himself on the way he can set up a motor cycle's suspension or tune an engine for perfect carburation, did not consciously learn how to race a motor cycle. The opposite happened, in fact, as it was his natural feel for a racing engine that triggered his first racing experience.

"It had never really occurred to me to go racing myself. My Dad always ran Bultacos for other riders. He'd had people like Read and Ivy riding for him and I'd gone along with him since I was about five. When I was nine he taught me how to start a racing bike. I couldn't touch the ground but I'd sit on it as he pushed and I soon learnt the knack of getting the engine started. When I was eleven I was in the workshop with him rebuilding engines.

"With the beginning of '68 Dad had new Bultacos just as he did every year but he didn't have anyone to ride them, or even run them in. He was getting pretty disheartened with racing in general because the guys he'd had riding for him the previous year were always either crashing the bikes or wrecking the engines. His misfortune and lack of success had meant that I had lost interest in racing; I was into trials and I was working quite hard so I didn't have much time anyway. But without anybody else to do the job he suggested that I go down to Brands to run the bikes in. I certainly didn't think that riding a racing bike was the greatest because when I first had a go on a 50cc Derbi round Brands at the age of seventeen Ron Chandler came blasting past me on a 500 and I thought 'Jeez, this has got to be the worst thing in the world'. But anyway, I borrowed a set of leathers and went down and tootled around for the day, running the bikes in.

"The following day somebody who had been at the track phoned Dad up and said 'You should have seen Barry go, he was really quick'. So the next Wednesday Franco came down with me and we set about sorting out the jetting. I said it was too rich in the mid-range. It all seemed natural enough, perhaps because I'd been around racing bikes for so long. The thing that surprised Dad and I, though, was that I was quicker than the other guys Dad had had riding for him. So while we were thinking about who should ride for Dad, it dawned on him that perhaps I should have a go.

"We entered a club meeting at Brands on the 125 and the 250. The 125 wouldn't go at all in practice but we jetted it down and got it to run. I started the race about fourth, moved up to third, then second and was catching Mike Lewis who was leading. I went along the bottom straight into the left hander and just as I flicked it over for the right it locked solid, pitching me over the handlebars. I landed straight on my face and cut my chin. They carted me into the ambulance but I didn't want them to take me off to hospital so I got out and walked back to the pits. I can still see Dad's face now. He was standing at the entrance to the tunnel as I came walking out with blood smeared across my cheek. He said 'That's it, we'll load the bikes up. Let's go home' but I said 'Hang on, Franco, I'm Okay and there's still the 250 race'. So we stayed and after a bad start I finished third. Next time out we raced the 125 and a 350 and I won both.

"From then on I was hooked. It didn't take me long to get my international licence but from the May of that year – it was '68 – until almost the end of the season I went mechanicing on the Continent for Lewis Young. I learned a lot more about engines and racing in Europe. I went back to racing at the end of the season and I've enjoyed it ever since. In fact, I enjoy it more now because I understand it. I know what the bike wants but I'm still learning, still juggling with things like the fine balance between head angle and trail that is so crucial to the steering. Setting up the bike gives me as much pleasure as the actual racing."

It would be easy to form the opinion that to be a World Championship class road racer, one must have served a long apprenticeship of racing motor cycles, adjusting suspension, trying new frames, different wheel rims, tyres, brakes etc. What then of the rider who grows up racing production bikes where the regulations force him to ride the bike virtually as it comes from the showroom floor? Such a rider cannot develop a feel for the effect various adjustments have on machine performance and would have little cause to try and understand the reasons behind the way his motor cycle performs, or more likely misbehaves.

Graeme Crosby was brought up almost purely on a diet of production racing. When he first stepped on a racing machine at a full international level he gained a reputation for one who was more capable of riding a bike in what ever state it was given to him to a limit way above that which most others could attain. But then he joined the Suzuki Grand Prix team and his quick intelligence allowed him to use the experience of those around him. "The Japanese understand the way their suspensions are supposed to work – and they don't let you go too far wrong. You can come in from a practice session and ask them to increase the spring rate and then they'll look at their charts, work out the deflection you'll get on the suspension unit and the amount of wheel travel, and then

they'll tell you whether it keeps the suspension in its operating range. Or if not, what else you should do.

Franco Uncini leads Graeme Crosby and Kenny Roberts at Donington Park.

"That sort of experience has saved me from making a lot of mistakes that I'm sure I would have made as a privateer. You can go whacking on the pre-load on a spring until the bike throws you down the road and you'll probably never know why. I never had the chance to learn from my mistakes because I spent so much time riding production bikes and the way it's turned out that has been lucky. But if I wasn't protected by being a factory rider, I wouldn't have too much idea on how to set a motor cycle up. What riding production bikes did teach me early on was to explore the limits of the tyres and, I suppose, I also learned to ride around a machine's defects to a certain extent. But today's 500 Grand Prix bikes are so powerful and fast that if you haven't got them pretty nearly right, it's virtually impossible to be in the pace.

"The first thing I try and set up is the carburation because until you get that right I reckon it's impossible to set up the suspension. Getting a two stroke to run is all about carburation and that's why I don't find it as interesting as racing a four stroke. There's so much more to four stroke racing because of the greater complexity of the engine and I wish the Grand Prix class was four stroke. I do the World Championship because that's where all the best riders are

24

and it's the most important thing, but I really enjoy riding a four stroke more."

Unfortunately, of course, international racing is not just about enjoyment. If it was Graeme Crosby would still be racing in the TT in the Isle of Man, content to ride around at the speed he thought was safe which in itself would doubtless be faster than almost anyone else. But riding at that speed might not be enough to win every race and the pressure on Graeme as a works rider to win meant that he no longer felt he could race at a safe speed and still do the job expected of him. The whole question of safety in racing is an awkward subject to talk about because racing is intrinsically dangerous and so it is impossible to race at a totally safe speed on any track. On the other hand it's plainly ludicrous to race at twelve tenths on a circuit where any mistake is likely to kill you. The balance between danger and speed at various circuits is crucial to how fast any rider will be prepared to go and if he is honest with himself somewhere the rider must draw the line.

For Jon Ekerold the line includes racing at the TT. He sees it as a fairer test of skill than man-made circuits where works machines almost always dominate. Jon has long been known as one of the hard men of racing and has been unfortunate enough to sustain a good number of injuries during his career. But he views the danger he faces on a racing machine as an acceptable part of achieving success, which includes the 350cc World Championship in 1980. Sometimes when he talks about the risks there is the unmistakable flippant bravado: "If you're going to crash, then do it on the first lap because then you don't wear the engine out for nothing". And then the day before his show-down with Toni Mang in 1980 at the Nürburgring: "Crashing here is of no consequence, I've just got to win".

When talking seriously, Jon is none the less frank: "I certainly don't go out to race anywhere with the idea of falling off. That's not the object. As for different circuits, I think you can get hurt crashing anywhere. I might push my luck a little more on some of the man-made tracks because I know that if I run off the circuit I can ride back on again. Generally speaking, if you want to win you've got to go damn fast wherever it is. As for the TT, I certainly don't ride round there with very much in reserve. I suppose the difference is that if I don't absolutely know that I can get through the particular section at a certain speed, I won't try it just to see what happens.

"There are places like the approach to Kirk Michael and Handleys where I will brake twenty metres early, not because I don't trust my judgement but because if you should have a brake

Regarded by many as the "hard man" of motor cycle racing, Jon Ekerold won the 350cc World Championship in 1980 before changing to the 500cc class.

failure there I think you really would be dead.

"I never really think of myself getting killed but I know that racing is dangerous and it could happen. If it did, I think you would have to reckon on what I've done in life and not the length of it. I could have spent my time working from nine till five in a factory in total boredom and have never gone anywhere. But in doing what I do I've seen a good part of the world and have so much excitement and experience that I could never have had in other ways."

It is a fact of life that people, as they get older, see danger more clearly. Road racers are no different in this but if every rider started to go more slowly as he got older it would only be the impetuous youths who ever won any races. As a balancing factor, experience seems to make up for the lack of regard for personal safety.

Barry Sheene was never particularly noted for a devil-may-care attitude to his racing but in the first half of his career due to various reasons, including mechanical failure, he suffered some severe injuries and among them the infamous Daytona crash resulting in multiple fractures and internal injuries. But after ten years of Grand Prix racing he has all but eradicated falling off without losing any of his speed. "You eventually learn how fast it is possible to go and, especially at Grands Prix, you pace yourself for a race making a move at the right moment when the tyres are working well. Experience will help in setting up the bike properly; that is important because if your motor cycle handles better than anyone else's then you can go faster than them without falling off. That's the way I like to play it; I find it's easier on the body."

For the works rider the consequences of falling are pain and personal injury but the privateer must reckon on loss of earnings if he cannot race. By the time he has also counted the cost of repairs to his machine he is bound to see crashing as financially disastrous if nothing else. The brilliant Finnish privateer, Seppo Rossi, manages to score World Championship points against the works riders in the 500cc class. "In 1981 I finished fifteenth in the World Championship and because I have no sponsor I had to race very carefully. I never ever felt close to falling off; I couldn't afford to because I rely on my prize money from Grands Prix to live."

For a young rider who hopes to be on his way to the top, falling off is almost a necessary evil. He will always be riding at new circuits and trying new machines without the necessary experience to minimise the risks. For him, and riders like him, winning may be 90% mental attitude, believing that they are better than any other rider on the track, getting pumped up, as Kenny Roberts says. It is

Seppo Rossi proved that privateers could beat works riders but eventually the cost of doing so without assistance forced him to retire.

not surprising therefore that the climb of many riders' careers is interrupted by plateaux. They climb while they are successful, boosted by confidence, and able to ride to the full extent of their talent and experience. Then the temptation is to push themselves too hard, to go beyond what they have learned and they begin to fall off. A series of accidents dents their confidence and they draw back to what they know they can achieve, marking time for a while until their confidence revives.

Donny Robinson contested his first European Grand Prix season in 1982 with some success. Although not noted as a crasher he accepted that, as he worked his way to the top, falling off was a risk he had to take. "One of the main problems is machinery. You have to prove yourself on an inferior bike. That means riding it hard around the corners and always trying harder. Plus there are always new tracks to learn. Sometimes I have fallen off; it's certainly not the idea but it happens, right enough. I always sit down and analyse why it's happened and as long as I can work out why, it doesn't worry me. I aim to learn from my mistakes and not do it again. Thinking about things like that is important if you want to improve. When I get on the bike again it doesn't affect me; even if I have had a big crash it doesn't slow me down because I've worked it out and it shouldn't happen again."

A rider does not have to merely accept the fact that falling off hurts. He can increase his resistance to injury considerably by improving his state of physical fitness and as Grand Prix races are long, strenuous and often take place in hot climates, physical strength and stamina are very important.

If you follow a stiff fitness regime then there is little chance of carrying around excess weight in the form of fat. On the other hand you may not be a super lightweight either because there will be a certain amount of weight in muscle bulk. A very light rider will allow his machine to accelerate more quickly and in the small capacity classes this is important. But even on a 250 or a 350, and definitely on a 500, a reasonable amount of weight need not be a disadvantage. Rider weight is at least movable: hanging off the machine in a corner or sliding forwards or backwards when accelerating or braking will move the centre of gravity to advantage.

Injury does not just affect the rider physically; equally importantly he can suffer mentally. Even if he is physically fit to race, his confidence may have been damaged so that he cannot race on top form. It may be that the rider bounces back after injury and appears to be racing flat out but he may not be able to start the machine as quickly, or his riding style could be affected by a stiff joint, for instance. More likely he fears that a fall will cause him immediate greater damage. A loss of performance can soon lose a rider his sponsorship, perhaps the backing of the tyre companies, mechanics and everyone else essential to a first class race effort. It becomes a vicious spiral as poor race results lead to inferior machinery and hence even worse results. Breaking out of the spiral requires an unshakable belief in one's own ability.

Alan North knows about the ups and downs of top class racing as he was at the top of the 350cc class in 1977 when he won the Italian Grand Prix and finished ninth in the World Championship. That winter he badly fractured his leg in a trail bike accident in South Africa and he missed the following season as the nasty injury was slow to heal. He returned to the Grand Prix circuit in 1979 but it took time to get back into his stride. The leg was still a nuisance when push starting the bike and he could not afford to fall on it again. His motor cycle was not competitive and as he failed to produce results to match his previous performance there was no sponsor willing to supply him with new machinery. It was down to Alan to pull himself back to the front.

"When you're on top, everyone wants to help you. When you're on the bottom and you really need it there's very little offered. I've

Alan North knows how it feels to have one foot on the summit of the sport, only to be kicked down to the bottom of the mountain and have to start again.

always felt confident in my own ability to ride fast but it's difficult to prove it, especially now as there are so many top class riders. When I came over in '75 there were only five or so fast riders and even though I didn't have the latest bike I didn't have too hard a time. I finished eleventh in my first Grand Prix, the Dutch, on my TD2. Wildan, a Dutch company, bought me a new bike for the following year and I soon began to get results.

"When you've been at the top and then had a set-back it's very difficult to regain that confidence in what you can achieve. One time, when you went out to practice, you knew you'd be in the top five, and then, there you are scratching to try and get in the top twenty. It's hard to make the adjustment. Then during a race somebody will come past on a faster bike so you outbrake them at the end of the straight. Then they re-pass you on the next lap, you out brake them again, then they pass you on the straight. After a while it's very tempting to stay in the position you are and let them get away.

"I know I can ride fast though and I keep trying. I certainly enjoyed my racing a lot more in '80 and '81 than I did in '79. I certainly still enjoy riding a motor cycle at speed but you have to think of it as a job and I worry more about what bikes I'll have to ride next year than I did when I first came to Europe."

World Champions attract a lot of attention.

Some distance away from Alan North's concern as to what motor cycles he might ride in the coming season, are the highly paid professionals like Barry Sheene who worry as to whether they can afford a light aircraft or a helicopter. But even Sheene has had his ups and downs. Two 500cc World Championships were followed by two unhappy years with Suzuki and then a lean season as a privateer on production Yamahas. Such is Sheene's total professionalism that not only has he remained a first class rider but he is as sought after by the media five years after winning his second World Championship as he was at the time. Not only does this mean that he continues to make a great deal of money out of road racing, but it ensures that the factories are more than happy to supply him with first class machinery, almost irrespective of whether he is World Champion or not. For this reason his professionalism and the way he promotes himself cannot be completely divorced from his performance on the track. While some riders can win a Grand Prix one weekend and be forgotten the next, Sheene's personality helps his fame and his results to endure.

There was the little girl who came looking for him in the pits at Silverstone in 1980. Barry was sitting beside his machine, pondering on what to do. Should he use the new, semi-works engine, a Roberts cast-off in the standard frame or in the Harris frame. The pressure was on: he had been narrowly beaten by Roberts at Silverstone the year before in front of a huge television audience. He desperately wanted revenge. The little girl found him and, obviously oblivious of the thoughts weighing heavily upon him, she announced herself: "Hello, I'm Karen. I've sent you cards four times for your birthday and you've never replied". Sheene was actually lost for something to say for a second but then seized her firmly round the waist and sat her on his knee. "Oh didn't I? Sorry love." That, and a smile was quite enough. The autograph he gave was a bonus and after a few minutes the little girl disappeared into the throng. Sheene retired before half the race was run but because little girls convince their Dads or brothers to buy Yamahas, Sheene remains one of the most valuable sportsmen in Britain.

As an ambassador for motor cycling throughout the world, it helps that he speaks Spanish, French and Italian fluently, with a smattering of enough other languages to get by wherever he might be. It's no exaggeration to say he meets kings and princes and appears on television and at dinners carrying himself off with the casual charm that makes him difficult to dislike. It is a long way from the club road racer with fingernails broken and dirty from working on the bike all night, but make no mistake it is a very important part of being a successful, professional road racer.

No-one is suggesting that Barry Sheene is all sweetness, and anyway, don't nice guys finish last? Surely it is necessary to dislike somebody to want to beat them so much that you risk everything to nudge your front wheel under their right elbow as you peel into a corner at 130 miles an hour. But it does not seem to be that way. By and large, riders live in harmony in the paddock, parking their motor homes together and sharing a barbecue or taking rooms in the same hotel, or playing golf together between test sessions. How then does the rider work up the necessary aggression to push back the natural boundaries of fear and self-preservation. Every rider probably has his own answer but Graeme Crosby explains what helps him to get in the right frame of mind.

"The best thing for me is to have a cross word with one of my mechanics just before the start of the race. Nothing major, just something to put me on edge, something to help me work up my aggression. Once the race has started I will focus that aggression on whoever's in front. I say to myself 'I'll get him, I'll have the b . . . .!!' It doesn't matter who it is but it helps me to catch them. But you don't have to dislike somebody to want to beat them. The guy I'd say I get on best with is Kork, but if it came to the last corner and we're fighting for the lead at a Grand Prix there would be no 'After you, I'll let you win this race'. But after we'd crossed the line it would be a hell of a rush to take our helmets off to stick our tongues out at each other and say 'Hee, hee, hee, I beat you'."

2

Why motor cycles go round corners

The perfectly balanced grace of a motor cycle ridden at speed through the twists and turns of the race track is something that the enthusiast will never tire of. Anyone's first sight of racing machines in action is bound to strike the viewer with awe. The sheer speed is likely to exceed previous experience and the notion that man and machine can actually turn a corner at that pace is almost beyond belief.

Kork Ballington was virtually unbeatable on the twin cylinder Kawasakis.

When the watcher recovers from the initial assault upon his senses he is inevitably astonished by the incredible angle of lean accomplished by man and machine as they sweep through the turn. Even those of us who have been watching road racing for many years still flinch at the fairing scraping antics of some of the fastest riders. But if the young newcomer or the latest girlfriend ask 'Why don't they fall over?' many are inclined to answer with a knowing look or fob them off with a few platitudes about centrifugal force and friction.

Even if you race yourself you never completely overcome the surprise at a motor cycle's ability to lean over. It has occurred to me several times as I sweep through a long, fast corner to think with alarm just how far over the guy in front is leaning – and I'm gaining on him, so I must be leaning over further.

It is not even just the Sunday racers like myself who get a kick out of apparently defeating the laws of physics. Hardened professionals like Randy Mamola pass comment; he was discussing an epic struggle with Roberts and Lucchinelli after the 1981 German GP at Hockenheim and remarked to Kenny: "Did you see how far we were leaning over? It's best not to look down at the ground or you'll scare yourself stiff. You start to think to yourself 'How the hell can it lean over this far?'."

The fact of the matter is of course that the laws of physics are never cheated by the racing motor cycle. They are obeyed every second and the rider either through instinct or experience uses every one, balancing one physical principle against another to guide the machine along the desired course with the maximum

Roberts, hard at work on the Daytona banking.

possible speed. To do this he must balance the centrifugal force,[1] which tends to throw the rider and machine away from the centre of the corner, against the centripetal force which works in the opposite direction. The centripetal force acting toward the centre of curvature of the corner is provided by the machine's tendency to fall over once it has been leaned into the corner. Imagine sitting on a stationary machine and not even trying to balance; once the machine starts to fall to one side it requires a great deal of strength to stop it from falling over completely. The weight[2] acts downwards and, just like the caber tosser who runs forward to stop himself and the caber from falling flat, the motor cycle in motion turns towards the direction in which it is leaning to stop itself falling on its side. This turning towards the centre creates the centripetal acceleration but just as the caber tosser needs to grip the ground with the soles of his shoes to run forward, the motor cycle exerts the centripetal force through the grip of its tyres.

The downward force of the weight of the machine and the centrifugal force can be considered to act through the centre of gravity[3] of the combined body, that is man and machine. Consider the tyres and road contact patch as a hinge, so that there is no slip and the man and his motor cycle are free to lean, pivoting about that point. The weight of the rider and bike acts downward and that is balanced by the centrifugal force pulling outward, like two people pulling at the door handle from opposite sides of the door.

The weight of the bike and rider are constant but centrifugal force varies depending on the speed of the machine and the radius of the corner (fig. 1). Taking a tighter corner at a certain speed or a given corner at a higher speed creates more centrifugal force and this must be balanced by the weight. You cannot increase the weight in the middle of the corner, and even if you did the centrifugal force is, like weight, a product of the mass, and so that would also increase and you would have gained nothing.

What you can do is increase the effect of the weight. Think again of the static motor cycle. When you are sitting on the machine it requires only a little touch on the ground to keep upright as long as

---

1 In the strictest scientific sense centrifugal force does not exist, but it is a very useful concept described thus: a body constrained to move in a curved path reacts against that constraint with a force directed away from the centre of curvature of its path. That force is called centrifugal force. It is equal and opposite to the force that has caused it to deviate from the straight line. This is the centripetal force. They are both equal to the product of mass of the body and its centripetal acceleration. Its value is $\frac{mv^2}{r}$ where m is the mass of the body, v is the velocity and r is the radius of curvature.

2 Weight is a product of mass and gravity and always acts vertically downwards; its value is equal to mg where g is the acceleration of gravity: 32ft/sec^2 or 9.8 m/sec^2.

3 If you suspend a body from any point its centre of gravity can be determined by the fact that the weight pulls the centre of gravity (c of g) down to vertically below the point of suspension.

the bike doesn't stray far from the vertical, but if for some reason the bike has fallen well over to the side it requires a real effort to pull it up again. The effect of the weight is all down to the horizontal distance that the c of g has moved from the base of the machine, which is the tyre contact patch. The further over the machine goes the greater the distance and the greater the effect of the weight.

So to counteract the increase in centrifugal force the rider increases the effect of the weight by leaning further over. This has the added bonus of reducing the effect of the centrifugal force by reducing the vertical distance between the c of g and the hinge or

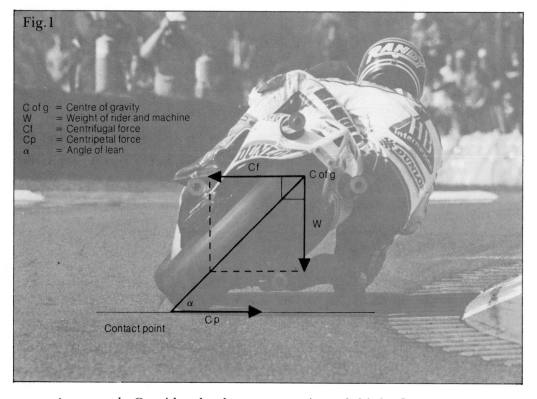

Fig. 1

C of g = Centre of gravity
W = Weight of rider and machine
Cf = Centrifugal force
Cp = Centripetal force
α = Angle of lean

tyre contact patch. Consider the door once again and think of two people pushing at it instead of pulling (pushing and pulling is the same as far as this explanation is concerned) except that one person is pushing the door at the handle and the other person on the other side of the door is pushing much closer to the hinge. Obviously the pusher at the handle has a great advantage because he is further from the hinge. Note that it is the distance measured vertical to the direction of the force that is critical in all these considerations.

There is a diagrammatic method of working out just what angle of lean is required to balance a machine of a certain weight against a certain centrifugal force. If you do a drawing and give the weight and centrifugal force lines of length comparable to their strength and mark those lines in the direction the forces act, then the sum or resultant of the two lines must point through the contact patch or hinge of the machine. Only when this resultant acts through that contact patch or base is the machine stable, with no tendency to swing to either side.

If you know the centrifugal force acting on the machine then you know the frictional force provided by the tyres because the centrifugal force must always be equal and opposite to the centripetal force (fig. 1) and that is exerted through the tyres. The simple law of friction[4] states that the friction is limited by the tyres and the weight of rider and machine. This means that the frictional force cannot be greater than the weight of bike and rider. Because the centripetal force is transmitted by the friction this in turn limits the centripetal and hence the centrifugal force to being no more than equal to the weight of the machine. If you apply these facts to our diagram (fig. 1) it means that both lines must be equal in length and therefore a motor cycle can never lean over more than 45 degrees to the vertical.

But this is simply not true in practice. Perhaps Mike Hailwood was the first rider to be pictured exceeding that magic figure, but certainly today's top stars do it all the time and appear to defeat the laws of friction. The answer really lies in the chapter on tyres, particularly pages 145-146. What happens is that two things work beyond the simple law of friction. Firstly the tyre rubber actually moulds around the grains of tarmac and this effectively raises and puts the frictional force above the weight. This means that the centripetal force can be greater than the weight and therefore the angle of lean goes past 45°.

Randy Mamola hangs off the seat which helps to move the centre of gravity to the inside of the corner and means that he doesn't have to lean the motor cycle quite so far over.

Secondly the tyres do track sideways as the motor cycle corners. Even before the tyre actually starts to slide the flexibility of the rubber allows it to walk sideways slightly. Under acceleration the rear tyre will walk outwards and actually steer the motor cycle round the corner. This situation is called over steer and as the drive of the machine is towards the inside of the corner it is adding to the centripetal force and hence the angle of lean can be greater. If the front tyre does not grip properly and if it does not follow the desired course then it is said to under steer.

Although the technicalities up to this point describe fairly

4 $F = uC$ where F is the frictional force, u is the coefficient of friction for the two surfaces (in this case rubber and tarmac) and C is the normal contact force. C is the force exerted upwards on the body by the ground, it is equal and opposite to the weight. u cannot be more than 1. This means that in the simple case F is limited by the weight of the rider and machine.

Sometimes even Randy Mamola cannot believe the angle of lean that he achieves. "You'd better not look down at the ground or you begin to think that you're about to fall off."

completely the rules that control the motion of a motor cycle through a curve there is another principle that is very important to the way the front wheel steers and also has a bearing on the way the machine tracks through the corner. The principle is that of gyroscopic precession.[5]

As the wheels of the motor cycle spin in, what we shall call, a clockwise direction when viewed from the right hand side, the action of leaning the machine to the left causes the front wheel to turn to the left and this helps a rider to steer into a corner.

Depending on the direction of rotation of the crankshaft, accelerating or decelerating in the middle of a corner will cause the motor cycle to either lean over further or stand more upright. The effect of the crankshaft, because it is normally, to a certain extent, cancelled out by the rotation of the clutch in the opposite direction, is generally considered less important than the rotation of the wheels which always help the motor cycle lean over when accelerating. This explains the frightening feeling that you experience if you change into neutral while rushing into a corner. It is very difficult to make the machine turn because you cannot accelerate and gain the advantage of gyroscopic precession.

Another factor which helps the motor cycle turn the corner under acceleration is the tendency for the engine to pull itself around the rear sprocket. The engine pulls on the top run of the chain and this of course turns the rear wheel. But every action has an equal and opposite reaction so that pull also tends to pull the engine and the rest of the machine around the wheel in the opposite direction. When the motor cycle is leaned over in cornering, that action pulls the machine towards the centre of the corner and helps it go round. Decelerating puts the tension into the lower run of the chain to the opposite effect.

The effect of chain tension, which is sometimes referred to as 'climbing the sprocket', is most easily seen when the motor cycle accelerates hard out of a corner and lifts its front wheel in the air. Pulling a "wheelie" is accomplished not only by the chain pulling on the sprocket but also by the couple[6] created by the forward thrust of the rear wheel working against the mass of the machine which tries to resist the acceleration. The couple turns the motor cycle raising the front wheel in the air. As the front wheel rises the effect of the couple increases because the centre of gravity gets higher

Barry Sheene brakes hard for the Donington Park chicane. His weight and that of the machine is thrown forward onto the front wheel but already his right knee is sticking out as he slides off the seat moving the centre of gravity to the inside for the corner.

---

5   A body spinning about its axis like a wheel or crank shaft exhibits a desire to maintain the same orientation of the axis. If the axis is forcibly turned in one plane it will automatically also turn in the plane that is mutually at right angles to the plane of rotation and the plane of forced axis rotation.

6   A couple is created when two forces act on an object from opposite sides but are not exactly opposed. This places a turning movement, or effect, on the object.

Jean-Francois
Baldé has that
relaxed style
which makes him
look as if he could
go fast all day
and all night; he
can.

above the rear wheel and at the same time the effect of the weight acting downwards is decreased as the centre of gravity gets closer to the vertical line over the base, or rear tyre contact patch. This means that once the front wheel has been raised high in the air, very little acceleration is required to keep it there. Closing the throttle will bring the front wheel down to the ground and using the engine as a brake as you change down for a corner uses the pull on the bottom run of the chain to push down on the front.

Another factor which adds weight to the front of the machine under braking is the torque reaction[7] (fig.2). This again depends upon the direction of rotation of the crankshaft. If it rotates clockwise, torque reaction under acceleration will be anti-clockwise and under deceleration, clockwise. Of course the opposite is true of anti-clockwise crankshafts. So you can see that the direction of crankshaft rotation and its associated torque reaction is a contributory factor to wheelies under acceleration and weight transference under deceleration.

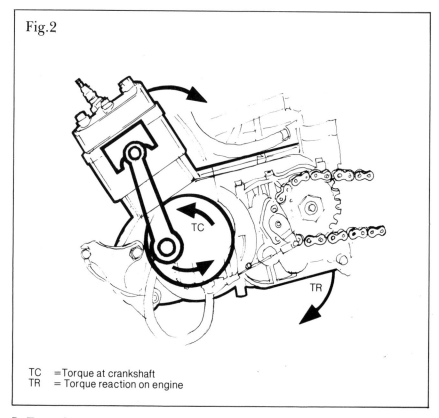

Fig.2

TC = Torque at crankshaft
TR = Torque reaction on engine

---

7 Torque is a turning force, experienced by a body when an effort is applied at a distance from its centre of rotation. An engine exhibits a torque reaction because the effort of turning the crankshaft is felt by the engine in the opposite direction. That is because every reaction has an equal and opposite reaction.

A far larger effect on forward weight transference is the pull on the bottom run of the chain and here riding style makes a great deal of difference. A rider who uses the gearbox and engine under braking will put more weight on the front because of chain pull. A rider who only uses the brakes, particularly the front brake, and has the clutch pulled in under braking obviously does not exert any pull on the chain. Under the heaviest braking, however, the rear tyre is barely in contact with the ground so no braking of the rear wheel, either by the rear brake or the engine, has any real effect.

Above all other considerations, the cause of weight transference under braking is the deceleration of the mass itself. This can best be explained by drawing a vector diagram[8] with a line that represents the weight of the machine which acts downwards, and another line representing the resistance to the applied braking force which acts horizontally (fig.3). As force always equals mass × acceleration and the mass, in this case, is the man and the machine, the vectors in the diagram are proportional to the acceleration of gravity (the weight)

Fig.3

C of g = Centre of gravity
W = Weight of rider & machine
Bf = Breaking force or deceleration
R = Resultant of W and Bf

8   A vector is a line whose sense, direction and length represent another value i.e. a force or speed.

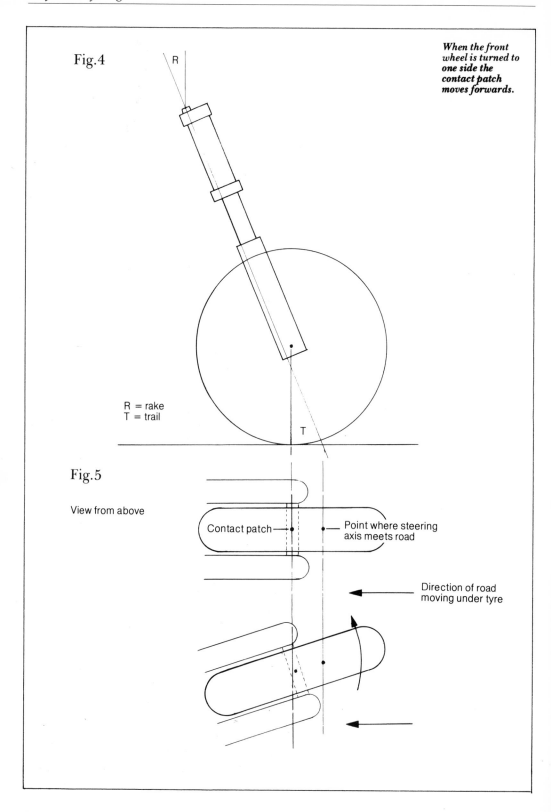

Fig.4

R

When the front wheel is turned to one side the contact patch moves forwards.

R = rake
T = trail

T

Fig.5

View from above

Contact patch

Point where steering axis meets road

Direction of road moving under tyre

and the deceleration of braking (the braking force). The resultant of these two vectors points forwards towards the tyre contact patch and this is the direction to which the weight is effectively being transferred.

If the resultant points farther forward than the front tyre contact patch, then the motor cycle will start to rotate about the front tyre contact patch and the rear tyre will come off the ground. In fact, the rear tyre will leave the ground before that point occurs because of the tremendous spinning momentum of the front wheel. As the brake calipers grab the front discs to stop them spinning, the calipers themselves are forced forward. This force of rotation about the front wheel spindle helps pull the back wheel into the air.

As we have seen, braking, accelerating and cornering on a motor cycle is largely a matter of weight transference. A two-wheeled machine with a front wheel that can turn to the left or right might almost steer itself and indeed, to a certain extent, motor cycles do. Riders often travel in a straight line and even corner with hands off the handlebar but they need some assistance from the front steering to provide stability. A machine with a vertical steering head, where the front tyre's contact patch is vertically below the steering stem, has no inbuilt stability at all. The very slightest force (for example, a small stone in the road) will turn the wheel to the left or the right. To provide the steering system with a self-centring action that gives it a natural, straight-on tendency, the steering head is inclined back at an angle. This puts the tyre contact patch some distance to the rear of a line drawn through the steering head (fig.4).

Now consider the motor cycle when it is rolling forwards. Turning the front wheel to the left or the right moves the contact patch outside the centre line of the machine (fig.5). The drag of the tyre on the road attempts to push the contact patch towards the rear. The only way that the contact patch can go rearwards is if it swings back behind the steering head. This provides the self-centring action. The self-aligning tendency is greater the further the contact patch lies behind the steering axis. The construction of the tyre itself also contributes to steering stability (see chapter 6).

Typically, trail on a racing motor cycle will be about 4½" (140mm) but there are other factors, such as wheelbase, which also affect stability and the trail may be varied. Short trail machines are quick to steer but may not be very stable, having a tendency to "shake their head". Long trail machines are normally very stable but may be cumbersome and slow to turn. Here rider preference and ability have an effect upon the steering geometry, i.e. the rake and trail, that he requires. Harris Performance Products build frames for both Grand Prix winners and inexperienced Club racers. Steve Harris explains: "A rider like Sheene wants a bike that is very quick to steer. He doesn't mind if it shakes its head a bit as he realises that he can't have both. A Club rider wants a machine that is more predictable: he doesn't want to feel that it might get out of control even if the stability means that he has to put in more effort to get the bike round the corner."

To a certain extent the rider might have to supply the turning force to overcome the self-centring action of the steering to hold the motor cycle on line in the turn. If perfectly designed, though, the machine can have a neutral steering feeling, thanks to the effect of the steering rake. The rake actually causes the centre of gravity of the machine to be lowered as it is turned to one side or the other. This can more easily be seen with the extreme steering geometry of the Chopper which has a very exaggerated head angle, or rake. Turning the handlebar lowers the front wheel spindle and hence the centre of gravity of the whole machine. You can imagine that, once lowered, a certain force is required to raise the centre of gravity again. So if the steering geometry of the machine is finely matched, the self-centring action of the wheel is actually balanced against the force required to raise the steering head. This means that once a turn is initiated it will be continued without further effort.

Initiating the turn is something that the motor cyclist does without thinking but it is quite a tricky principle to grasp. It is no good saying that you merely lean into the corner because the principle of every action having an equal and opposite reaction means that if the rider's weight is put to the right it can only be done by pushing the weight of the machine to the left, and you end up with the combined centre of gravity still in the same place. What actually happens is that to turn left you push forward slightly on the left hand handlebar, turning the wheel in the wrong direction. With the rider's handlebar pressure acting against the self-centring action of the wheel, the tyre steers the front of the machine to the right while the combined mass of man and motor cycle tries to carry straight on. This results in the machine beginning to fall to the left and once this fall to the left has begun the front wheel will naturally turn in to the left as the handlebar pressure is released.

If the rider wishes to come out of the corner quickly to straighten up, he must pull on the left handlebar, or push on the right, which turns the front wheel into the corner, upsetting the equilibrium[9] again and causing the motor cycle to 'fall' upright. The pressure

9 Equilibrium is the state in which the resultant of forces acting on a body is zero.

the rider puts on the handlebar is very slight and often done without thought. It becomes most apparent on machines with a lot of trail which are heavy to steer or when the motor cycle is moving very fast and the gyroscopic effect of the front wheel tends to keep the machine on a steady course.

The stability of the motor cycle is not only affected by the trail but also by the position of the centre of gravity. If the centre of gravity is further forward, a greater proportion of the machine's weight is carried on the front wheel and by increasing the pressure on the contact patch the self-centring effect of the steering is increased. This could be considered an advantage, but if too much weight is taken off the rear wheel its grip on the road is reduced.

Under heavy braking, the transference of weight onto the front helps increase the stability at a time when compression of the front forks has reduced the rake and trail (fig.6). This explains why it is better not to have 100% anti-dive, but rather, perhaps, 50%. If the forks collapse by half their travel, the trail will be reduced but the self-centring action is restored by the increased pressure on the contact patch.

Riders sometimes make use of the fact that increased weight on the front wheel helps stability by pulling themselves forward, leaning on the petrol tank around fast bumpy corners. They do this knowing that taking the weight off the back wheel might cause it to step out, but this is preferable to having a front wheel that is uncontrollable because it is either not in contact with the ground, or has self-centring factors that are not sufficient. The rider moving his weight forward or back is usually barely perceptible but everyone can see the rider who hangs off the seat in a corner, moving his weight inside the machine. This is a useful ploy as it enables him to balance the centrifugal and centripetal forces etc. while keeping the motor cycle itself more upright. This means that if his cornering clearance is limited, the rider can increase the angle of lean attained by the centre of gravity without increasing the angle of lean of the motor cycle itself.

Not all riders find it necessary to hang off their bikes, however. Mick Grant, for instance, always sits immobile, in line with his machine but perhaps he developed his riding style when tyres gave less grip and when ground clearance was not such an acute problem. There are still anomalies, though: riders like Boet van Dulmen who push their bike down into the corner while keeping their bodies more upright.

The way a rider sits on his machine not only affects the weight distribution but also the aerodynamic[10] characteristics. When Kork

10 Aerodynamics is part of the mechanics of fluids, dealing with the dynamics of gases. In particular it studies the forces which act on a body moving in air.

Randy Mamola lifts the front wheel of his Suzuki at Jarama.

TO13760

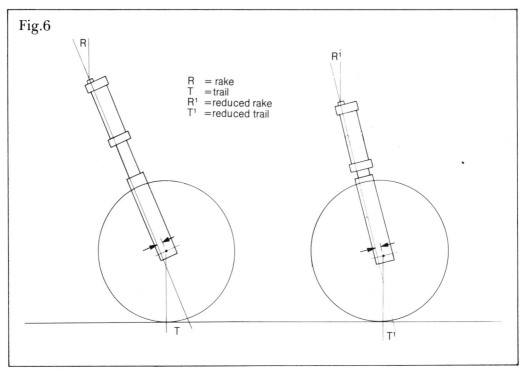

Fig.6

R = rake
T = trail
R¹ = reduced rake
T¹ = reduced trail

Ballington was riding the works 250 and 350 Kawasakis he found that the smaller machine particularly was affected by how well he tucked himself in behind the fairing: "I could get another three or four hundred rpm in top gear by making sure that my elbows and knees were tucked behind the fairing." In this respect his main competitor, Gregg Hansford, was unlucky in that he was too tall to get properly tucked away.

When the front forks are compressed the steering trail is reduced

The whole question of aerodynamics and streamlining[11] hinges on the fact that a motor cycle, or any other speeding body, has to push the air out of the way as it passes and it must then allow the air to reform behind. The energy required to do this is provided by the motor cycle's engine; it is the power of the engine against the resistance of the air which limits the motor cycle's top speed and not its weight, or any other consideration.

The perfect shape for air penetration at speeds normally attained by motor cycles is an elongated tear drop where the blunt end gently parts the air and the tapered tail draws it back together. Unfortunately the bike and the rider, even with a racing fairing, bears little relationship to the perfect shape and is not much more aerodynamic than a brick. The FIM regulations that govern motor cycle design to a great extent limit the aerodynamic possibilities.

11 The shaping of a body so that it passes through air, or any other fluid, with the least possible disturbance.

This shows the frontal area of Jacques Bolle's 250 Yamaha. To this must be added the top of his helmet which will protrude slightly above the screen.

They state that the front wheel must be visible from both sides, except for the use of a normal mudguard as must the rider except for his forearms. The seat or tail fairing cannot extend beyond the rear tyre and that 180° of the rear wheel must be visible behind a line drawn vertically through the spindle (see chapter 3).

The rules were not always so restrictive: up until 1957 they allowed the use of so-called dustbin fairings which created a much better frontal shape, closer to the tear drop nose. They were banned because only the works teams could afford to develop them

The Bolle brothers' 1982 machines were well streamlined with careful consideration given to the important tail section. The cooling air from the radiator is ducted out through the side of the fairing instead of being left to find its own way as is often the case.

and while the bikes were getting faster by some 15 mph, the brakes were overheating because they were enclosed.

As things stand now the front wheel presents a very disturbing nose and all that can be done is to create the best fairing possible behind and above it. Kawasaki made several attempts to make the front mudguard of the KR500 work as a piece of streamlining, not so much to improve the motor cycle's penetration of the air but to improve the flow of air into the radiator. In 1981 their front mudguard was called streamlining by the opposition and the

Christian Sarron, riding a beautifully faired 750cc Yamaha, especially streamlined for the high speed banking at Daytona. The front might be perfect but the tail section needs more attention.

company modified it before coming into conflict with the scrutineers over its legality.

It is not just the shape of the front of the machine that matters but its size or frontal area.[12] The smaller the frontal area, the smaller the hole it punches in the air and the less energy absorbed with the machine's passing. That, though, is only the beginning, for the disturbance made by the motor cycle is felt much further afield than just the air molecules that are immediately in its path. In a perfectly streamlined body, the molecules which are pushed aside as the body passes through are pushed further and further away from their original position until the widest part of the body has passed. Then they are drawn back together to take up their former positions after the tail of the body has passed. This smooth displacement and replacement is rarely attained because the molecules are kicked aside with such force that they hurl away from the side of the body creating a partial vacuum in the machine's wake. This vacuum sucks at the back of the motor cycle and slows it down. The air molecules come rushing in to fill the vacuum, but the drain on the engine's power is considerable.

The suction on the back of the body is called pressure drag; another type of drag is created by the molecules of air as they pass across the body's surface. The layer of molecules that are actually touching the body adhere to it and assume its velocity. The next layer of molecules roll over the first and move slightly slower; the third layer moves a little slower still and so on until, at some distance from the streamlined surface, the molecules do not move forward at all although they still may be pushed sideways by the passing of the machine. Those which assume all or a portion of the machine's velocity are called the 'boundary layer'. The friction generated by each molecule moving relative to the next is called 'skin friction' and this also detracts from a motor cycle's speed.

At the nose of the machine the boundary layer is thinnest because the pressure of the machine moving forward compresses it. Past the nose the boundary layer expands and in a non-perfectly streamlined body there will come a point when the layers of molecules no longer flow smoothly over each other but break up into turbulence. This causes increased drag; the point at which the boundary layer becomes turbulent depends on the speed of the body, its shape and surface roughness. If the tail of the machine reduces in section too quickly then the boundary layer will break contact with the surface altogether, creating a large vortex, or wake, and increasing the pressure drag mentioned earlier. Even

12 This is the area of the machine and rider's silhouette when viewed from the front.

though the boundary layer will certainly at some time become turbulent, if it can be kept in contact with the machine's surface the minimum pressure drag will be created. As it is the pressure drag which in the case of a motor cycle is by far the largest proportion of the resistance to forward motion, the tail of the motor cycle is much more important than the front when it comes to streamlining. In the front the boundary layer will always be kept in contact with the streamlining by the pressure created by forward motion. Skin friction is only of considerable importance in very long, well streamlined bodies like the cigar-shaped, land speed record attempt machines.

The shape of the object largely dictates the drag co-efficient, or Cd, which is so useful when discussing the relative shape of several bodies because it ignores their relative size. Cd is the sum of the pressure drag and skin friction and is measured in wind tunnel tests by using either a full size machine or a scale model. The object is placed on pads in the floor and air is blown over it at a speed comparable to the operating range of the vehicle. The pads are instrumented to feel the pressure exerted on the body by the air. Knowing the frontal area of the body, the Cd can be calculated. $Cd = \frac{D}{.0026 \, V^2 A}$ where D is the aerodynamic force in pounds, V is the speed in mph and A is the frontal area in square feet. $.0026V^2$ is the force that air exerts against a flat plate as it is pushed through the air at velocity V. When this is multiplied by the cross sectional area A, it compares the body with the flat plate of the same frontal area. By turning the equation around the force needed to push along a body of known drag coefficient at a given speed can be calculated: $D = .0026 \, V^2 \, Cd \, A$.

A slender tear drop may have a drag coefficient (Cd) of 0.15 and, even with a blunt nose, it is likely to be 0.16. The motor cycle does not compare very favourably: the average racing bike is probably between 0.4 and 0.5 though the factories that have tested their racing machines have kept the results a secret. The cause of the inefficiency is the critical tail area as the FIM regulations prevent any really effective tail streamlining.

Another important factor is the 'slenderness ratio'. This is the ratio between the length and the width of the object. The longer a body can be the nearer it comes to the ideal tear drop but in the racing motor cycle the length is dictated by the wheelbase, and this must allow the machine to corner in a competitive fashion. So, as the length cannot be increased significantly, the motor cycle's width should be decreased so that the slenderness ratio works to advantage.

At the very least the fairing should continue past the machine's

widest point so that they start to taper in before their trailing edges. This means that the air molecules are started on the converging path. A surprising number of racing machine fairings are still diverging when they are cut short and this sends the boundary layer spinning off in power-sapping vortices and greatly increases the disturbance the machine makes as it passes. Although a large proportion of the air flow goes around the sides of the motor cycle, and that is most affected by the machine's fairing, some goes over the top of the screen and the rider. When positioning the seat and the handlebars, most riders consider only their comfort. It would make sense if they gave more consideration to the air flow down their backs. Often the line of the rider's back is too steep for the air to stand any chance of maintaining contact down to the tail fairing. Were the rider to adopt a more crouched position the frontal area would be reduced, the slenderness ratio would be improved and

Ricardo Tormo was supreme at 50cc racing and the same rules apply even though the smallest capacity class is 80cc.

the shape of the rider's back would be more conducive to smooth air flow and reduced turbulent drag.

If the rider does not make the very best possible aerodynamic shape not only is he slowing himself down but he is also making a larger low pressure area behind which allows an ensuing rider to slip stream.[13] Depending on the speed of the machine, a following motor cycle may pick up its slip stream some 10 or 15 feet behind and be drawn along considerably faster than its own top speed.

Ricardo Tormo, 80cc ace, is one rider who does pay a good deal of attention to aerodynamics even at the expense of his comfort: "I normally wear a pair of boots that are a size too small; they may pinch a bit but they allow me to get tucked well away. Everything is important: gloves, helmet and of course leathers. I do not like

13 This refers to the following of one machine close behind the other so that the tailing machine is drawn along in the leader's aerodynamic wake, or slip stream.

wearing too many patches and letters on the back of my leathers because I think it disturbs the air flow."

The rider's seating position and the curve of his back also affects the machine's behaviour under braking. Certainly as he sits up at the end of the straight he forms a useful air brake but a low pressure area generated on his back may tend to lift the machine off the ground, reducing the friction generated at the tyres, and therefore the braking effect. The problem of aerodynamic lift is by no means as great on a motor cycle as it is in a car because most of the air passes around the sides of a bike and not over the top but it cannot be ignored completely. Lift is generated in two ways. An aeroplane wing, moulded in the classic aerofoil shape (fig.7) generates lift because the top of the wing is more curved and the air is made to pass over a greater distance and hence travels at a greater speed than that passing under the wing. This causes a reduction in pressure over the top of the wing[14] and pressure which is maintained under the wing therefore gives it lift.

Looking at the side of a motor cycle it bears little relationship to

A wing profile generates lift and so do many other shapes.

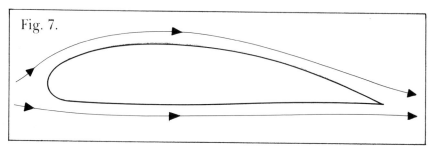

Fig. 7.

the profile of a wing. But if air is forced to pass over the machine at a greater speed than that which passes under it, lift will be generated. In fact the air flow underneath a motor cycle is so disturbed by the wheels that the flow over the top is hardly streamlined and it is unlikely that much lift is generated by this method.

The second way that lift is generated probably has more bearing on the situation. Air hitting the top of the screen is forced upwards and that creates a certain amount of down force but when that air is asked to turn around and head back down the rider to the tail fairing that creates a low pressure area even if it maintains contact as a streamlined flow. The lift generated never reaches the point of being able to lift the machine off the road, but effectively reducing the weight of the machine as it does cannot help stability.

14 Air pressure is generated by the air molecules which bounce around in random movement. As they bump into a body it feels the pressure. If the air molecules are made to pass over a body at twice the speed it will feel half the number of bumps and hence half the pressure.

Creating down force by the use of inverted wings etc. has been banned by the FIM and, in any case, they would have one disadvantage because, although it might help high speed stability, such devices would work against the machine as it was leaned past 45°. Then they would tend to push the machine away from the centre of the corner.

In the smallest classes designers using the 50cc and 80cc engines have sought to reduce the frontal area by raising the base of the fairing. This makes sense but in the 500cc class, with the large engines and wide tyres, another solution has been sought. The engine must be placed low in the frame to keep the weight down and designers have used the fairing to fill in the gap between the front and back wheels as much as possible. This is a good idea because there is little point in having the front wheel part the air only to make the rear wheel repeat the process. The well-designed fairings extend forwards at the front to a point as close as possible behind the front tyre (page 60).

One area that is given very scant thought by fairing designers is the passage of air through the fairing. Cooling air must pass through the radiator and this air, once warmed, should not be allowed to mix with the air drawn into the engine as hot air produces less power. The air that has passed through the radiator could usefully be used to fill in some of the low pressure areas behind the machine but in fact it is merely left to wander out as it chooses.

Because a motor cycle is always a compromise and no-one has a completely unlimited budget to spend, there will inevitably be a place for the clever engineer who has new ways of using materials or realises that perhaps an old idea can find a new use.

3

Rules and Regulations

Motor cycle racing bodies belonging to the Fédération Internationale Motocycliste (FIM)[1] run their International class races according to its rules. National regulations may vary but, in most cases, follow the FIM code closely. Founded in 1904, the rules have evolved over the years to keep pace with technical developments, by and large, although there are some anomalies in this area. This chapter is only the author's interpretation of the regulations that appear in Appendices 01 and 022 of the FIM Sporting Code. Dimensions in the regulations are given in metric units and have been converted here only for convenience.

General machine specification

Racing is divided into capacity classes and these are:

> 0cc to 80cc
> 80cc to 125cc,
> 175cc to 250cc,[2]
> 250cc to 500cc.

Capacity classes for the Formula TT, based on road engines, are:

	2 stroke		4 stroke	
	Over	up to	over	up to
Formula TT1	350	500	600	750
Formula TT2	250	350	400	600
Formula TT3	125	250	250	400

Engine capacities are calculated by the formula $\frac{D^2 \times 3.1416 \times C}{4} \times$ number of cylinders where D is the bore and C is the stroke. This only holds true in the case of the normal combustion engine, whether two stroke or four stroke. For a rotary engine, which is classified as a four stroke, the capacity is calculated $\frac{2 \times V}{N}$, where V is the total capacity of all chambers comprising the engine and N is the number of turns of

---

1 FIM, 19 ch. William-Barbey, CH-1292 Chambésy, Switzerland. Tel: (022) 58 19 60/61. Telex: Fedmoto CH 27321.
2 The 350 World Championship was last run in 1982 and was open to four cylinder engines with six gears weighing no less than 95kg. They had blue numberplates.

the engine completing one cycle in a chamber. For Wankel engines the capacity $= 2 \times V \times D$, where V is the capacity of a single chamber and D is the number of rotors.

Since 1949 supercharging has not been allowed in International road racing unless the combined capacity of the supercharger and the engine does not exceed the capacity limit for the class.

The number of cylinders and gears allowed in the various classes are as follows:

80cc	1 cylinder	6 gears
125cc	2 cylinders	6 gears[3]
250cc	2 cylinders	6 gears
500cc	4 cylinders	6 gears.

Road racing machines must be constructed to minimum weights when weighed without fuel and the addition of ballast to reach any of these minimum weight is forbidden. These weights are:

80cc	55kg
125cc	75kg
250cc	90kg
500cc	100kg.

One of the areas in which the FIM regulations appear to have missed the point is the restriction in the use of titanium[4] for they state 'For all motor cycles the use of titanium in the construction of the frame, the front forks, the handlebars, the swinging arms and the wheel spindles is forbidden. For wheel spindles, the use of light alloys is also forbidden.' It is odd that the FIM should ban these materials as, particularly in the case of titanium, there are many grades of titanium alloy just as there are many grades of steel alloy and it is ridiculous to suggest in a blanket statement that steel is safer to use than titanium as in general the latter has better fatigue[5] resistance.

The machine's handlebars must be at least 450mm (17in) wide or at least 400mm (15in) in the case of 50cc machines. The handlebars must be able to rotate 20° either side of centre; stops must be fitted to ensure a minimum clearance of 30mm (1.18in) between the handlebar and its levers and the petrol tank. Handlebar levers must be ball ended, throttles must be self closing and the ends of footrests must also be radiused.

One of the areas where racing motor cycles most often come into

---

3 For 1987 onwards the FIM state that the 125cc class will be restricted to single cylinder machines with six gears.
4 A metallic element, resembling iron, symbol Ti, widely used in aircraft manufacture, characterised by strength, lightness and corrosion resistance. A common element but difficult to extract and hence expensive.
5 Fatigue occurs in materials because of the repeated application of a stress cycle, commonly engine vibration, suspension movement, etc.

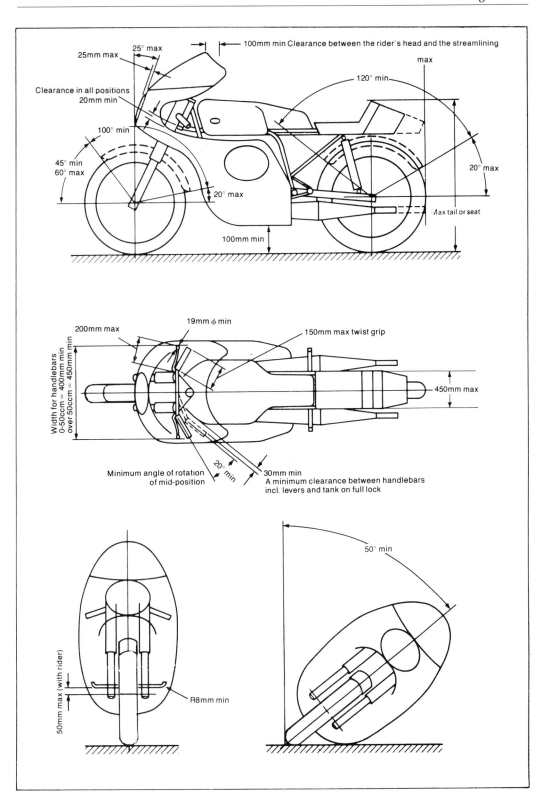

25° max

25mm max

100mm min Clearance between the rider's head and the streamlining

max

Clearance in all positions
20mm min

120° min

100° min

45° min
60° max

20° max

20° max

Max tail or seat

100mm min

200mm max

19mm φ min

150mm max twist grip

Width for handlebars
0–50ccm = 400mm min
over 50ccm = 450mm min

450mm max

Minimum angle of rotation
of mid-position

20° min

30mm min
A minimum clearance between handlebars
incl. levers and tank on full lock

50° min

50mm max (with rider)

R8mm min

conflict with the regulations is regarding streamlining. The regulations state that the front wheel, but not the tyre, must be clearly visible from each side. The streamlining cannot extend forward of the front wheel spindle or to the rear of the rear wheel spindle. The rim of the rear wheel must be clearly visible to the rear of this point. Seat fairings may extend beyond the rear wheel spindle but no further than the rear tyre. The rider must be, with the exception of his forearms, clearly visible from each side. There must be at least 20mm (0.79in) between the handlebars and levers and the streamlining. The ground clearance must not be less than 100mm (3.94in). The inclination of the fairing where the front number plate is fitted must not exceed 25° from the vertical.

Motor cycles, without the rider, must be capable of being inclined to an angle of 50° from the vertical without any part other than the tyre being in contact with the ground.

Number plates must form an elipse with minimum measurements 285mm (11.22in) by 235mm (9.25in). The minimum dimensions for the figures are 140mm (5.5in) high, 90mm (3.5in) wide with 25mm (0.98in) between the numbers. The English form of the numbers should be used which means, in theory, that Barry Sheene's Continental '7' is illegal. The colour coding for machine classes is as follows:

80cc	white background	black numbers
125cc	black background	white numbers
250cc	green background	white numbers
500cc	yellow background	black numbers.

The maximum fuel tank capacity for Grand Prix racing is 32 litres (7.04 galls), for TT Formula One 24 litres (5.28 galls), TTF2 20 litres (4.39 galls), and TTF3 18 litres (3.95 galls). Fuel must be contained in a single tank, securely fixed to the machine. Seat tanks and auxiliary tanks are forbidden. The use of temporary filling material to reduce the capacity of a tank is also not allowed.

Machines must be fitted with oil breather catch tanks, at least 250cc for gearboxes and 500cc for engine breathers. Oil drain plugs must be wired, as must oil supply pipes. Non-return valves must be fitted to petrol tank breathers.

For all road races the fuel used must be commercially available, i.e. sold at roadside service stations in one or more countries. No additions are allowed to this fuel with the exception of water or standard lubricants sold to the public. The only liquid engine coolants allowed are water or water mixed with ethyl-alcohol.

Noise emission from racing motor cycles is controlled to a maximum of 110dB/A, measured at an average piston speed of 13m/sec. for two stroke engines and 11m/sec. for four stroke

Ricardo Tormo lines up to have the noise level of his 50cc Bultaco tested. One scrutineer instructs him to hold the engine at a certain rpm and the other will go to the rear of the machine and point the noise meter at the exhaust pipe.

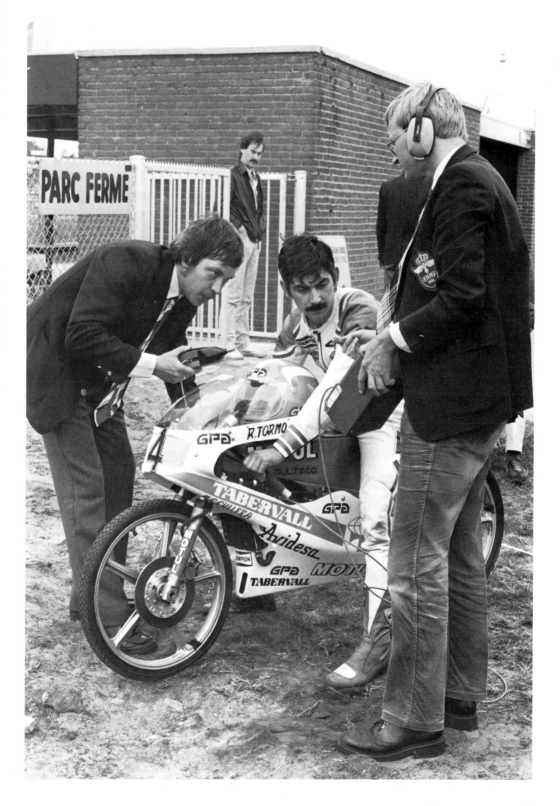

engines with a tolerance of +5dB/A for four strokes. Each engine must be marked with its stroke so that the correct rpm to achieve the required piston speed can be calculated using the formula $rpm = \frac{30p}{s}$ where p is the piston speed and s is the stroke. This means, in fact, that a 54mm stroke two stroke must be held at 7,222rpm for the noise test. The microphone is placed 500mm (19.69in) from the exhaust pipe outlet at an angle of 45°. The silencers are then marked and cannot be changed except for a spare silencer which must also be checked and marked.

The last thing this rider is thinking about is that his machine should legally be re-scrutineered before he rides it again.

Clothing

Riders must wear a complete leather suit of at least 1.2mm (0.05in) thickness. A non-leather material may be used if it is equal in performance to 1.5mm (0.06in) of cowhide in respect of fire resistance, abrasion resistance, co-efficient of friction, perspiration absorption and is non-toxic and non-allergic. The suit must have a double layer of leather or enclose plastic foam at least 8mm (0.31in) thick around the shoulders, elbows, both sides of the torso and hip joint, the back of the torso and the knees.

Undergarments must be worn if the suit is unlined and neither the undergarments nor the lining may be made of synthetic materials which may melt and harm the riders skin in an accident.

Boots must be worn to provide protection to a minimum height of 200mm (7.87in), made of leather or an equivalent material. Leather gloves must be worn.

Helmets must be worn, bearing an official stamp of approval of the rider's National Federation.

Grand Prix races

The World Championship Grands Prix are organised according to Appendix 022 of the FIM code. A Grand Prix event must contain at least four classes and one of these, in theory, should be the sidecar class. Exceptions to this ruling have to be approved by the Road Racing Commission. The Commission can approve non-World Championship races at a Grand Prix providing that the paddock is sufficiently large and that priority is given to the World Championship races.

The minimum number of starters for a race is 36, with at least 44 being allowed to practice. Riders are not allowed to take part in more than two races. Priority for entries must be given to firstly, the FIM grading lists and secondly, the National Federation grading lists. FIM grading list number 1 is the first ten riders from the previous year's World Championship. Places in the 80cc and 125cc class allow access to all classes up to 250cc. Places in the 250cc and 500cc class allow access to all solo classes. FIM list number 2 is for riders placed eleventh to fifteenth in the previous year's World Championship but allows access only to that class. List number 3 is drawn up by the FIM based on Continental Championships, consisting of in principle:

3 riders from the European Championship
2 riders from North America
2 riders from Latin America
1 rider from Australia
1 rider from Africa
1 rider from Asia.

The fourth list includes riders who have won points in the current year's World Championship. After these four lists have been satisfied, riders are accepted according to the National Federation lists, drawn up by the individual countries. The FIM number 3 grading list may receive additions halfway through the year if the FIM is informed by a rider's Federation of exceptional results in International races that year. The Federation's own grading list may be changed by that Federation during the season.

Practice for Grands Prix must be over at least four practice sessions with two separate sessions per day for each class. The total duration of practice must be at least two hours and twenty minutes and between two practice sessions on the same day there must be an

interval of at least three hours.

On the morning of the race day the organiser is recommended to allow ten minutes untimed practice for each class.

Grid positions are determined by practice times and if two or more riders have identical times, priority is given to the rider with the next best time in another session.

The distance for Grand Prix races are as follows:

	km	miles	km	miles
80cc	70	(43.50)	100	(62.14)
125cc	90	(55.92)	130	(80.78)
250cc	100	(62.14)	130	(80.78)
500cc	120	(74.57)	150	(93.21)

Grand Prix starting procedures are as follows: approximately thirty minutes before the start riders are called to the pre-race paddock. About fifteen minutes before the start, riders are brought onto the starting grid. Some ten minutes before the start, riders are sent off on a compulsory warm-up lap. As soon as the riders return to the grid, the Clerk of the Course will display as quickly as possible the three minute board at which time engines must be stopped and everyone but the riders leave the grid. Then a

Grand Prix races are not long enough for the bikes to need re-fuelling but at the Isle of Man TT and other long-distance events, quick fillers are used. The petrol enters the tank through the pipe pushed into a flap in its side and is vented via the tube placed in the top.

one minute board, a thirty second board and finally the signals indicating the start of the race are displayed.

Should it be necessary to stop the race due to an incident or climatic conditions, a red flag will be shown at the start and finish line and crossed yellow and oil flags shown at marshalls' posts.

If two laps or less of the race have been completed, the original start will be declared null and void and riders may re-start using either their original machine or a spare. If it is impossible to re-start the race no points will be awarded in the Championship. If more than two laps, but less than 75%, of the race has been completed, the race is considered to be in two parts. The race positions at the end of the first part are those of the lap preceding the stopping of the race and these are used for the grid of the re-start. The distance of the re-started race will be enough to complete the total race distance as originally intended. If a re-started race is impossible, half World Championship points will be awarded. If more than 75% of the race is completed before being stopped, it is declared a full race. The results stand as for the order on the lap before the race being stopped and full points are awarded.

Grand Prix prize money
Prize money is paid in Swiss Francs or an equivalent in a convertible currency based on the exchange rate published the week of the event. Winners' prize money is as follows:

80cc	4,000 Swiss Francs
125cc	5,900
250cc	8,450
500cc	14,850.

Monies decrease on a sliding scale down to 500 Swiss Francs for places beyond 26 for all classes.

4

In search of power

A typical engine
testing
arrangement. A
four cylinder,
disc valve engine,
in this case a
Barton Phoenix,
is tested using
only one of its
cylinders, the
others being
blanked off. This
obviously
simplifies tuning.

A racing engine must be designed to complete nearly half a million revolutions during the course of a Grand Prix. During that 45 minutes it might be subjected to a thousand gear changes and a 500 will drink most of the seven gallons (32 litres, 8.5 US gallons) it carries at an average consumption of 12 to 14 mpg (4 to 5 kpl, 10 to 12 mpg US).

The engine converts that effort into covering some 75 miles (120 km) at an average of 90mph (145kph). To do this the 500 will produce some 130bhp and, no less remarkable, an 80cc engine which produces only 30bhp still pushes the rider round at an average 90mph (144kph).

All the figures vary from race to race, from one machine to another and quoted horsepower is rather meaningless because unless the engines are all tested in the same dynamometer under controlled conditions the figures are not comparable. What matters is their performance on the race track and one of the fascinations of racing is that, despite the complications of rider ability, machine handling and tyres, the engineer still sees it as the ultimate test of his ability.

The various racing classes with capacity limits from 80cc upwards and levels of racing from amateur to Grand Prix give the engineer every chance to test his ability no matter what his financial resources. Although the 500 GP class is the ultimate contest and tickets to the winners enclosure are only bought by design teams with massive factory backing, the smaller classes are contested by individuals who have little sponsorship but still, thanks to their skill and ingenuity, produce and develop one-off machines of remarkable genius.

One thing almost all Grand Prix racing engines have in common is that they are two strokes,[1] as the only serious attempt to produce

1   An engine cycle completed in two strokes of the piston, i.e. one up and one down as the crank completes one revolution. During the upwards stroke the fresh charge is drawn into the crank case while the trapped charge is compressed in the cylinder. After combustion the piston descends on the power stroke allowing the spent gasses out through ports in the cylinder wall while the fresh charge is pumped from the crankcase to the same cylinder, via other ports, to become the trapped charge.

One of the most respected two stroke tuners in the world, Harald Bartol. Here he indicates the main bearing housing in his twin cylinder, disc valve racing engine.

a four stroke[2] since the withdrawal of MV from racing has been Honda whose NR500 never really matched the power production of the two strokes. Although the four stroke can burn the fuel it uses more efficiently even Honda's enormous research and development budget and very sophisticated use of advanced design and materials could not overcome the simple fact that the two stroke has twice the number of power strokes per crank shaft rotation compared with the four stroke. Given twice the capacity limit, 1000cc, several manufacturers have found it possible to produce four strokes with at least as much power as the 500cc GP two strokes.

The almost demonic search for more and more power that characterised the 500 GP battles of the 1970s seemed to wane at the turn of the decade as riders and engineers found that other factors

The only major class of racing dominated by four strokes is the Endurance championship. This is the 1981, World Championship-winning 1000cc Kawasaki.

2   An engine cycle completed in four piston strokes, i.e. two up and two down as the crank completes two revolutions. Stroke one is induction, drawing the charge into the cylinder, two compresses the gasses, after combustion the piston descends on the power stroke and then rises on the fourth exhaust stroke to expel the spent charge.

were preventing competitors from making use of the power available. The size, weight and power of the top works engines meant that tyres and frames were not coping with the demands made on them. The important change of direction occurred at the beginning of 1981 when Suzuki produced the third major variation of their RG500 that had won Barry Sheene the World Championship in '76 and '77. The Gamma engine was considerably smaller and lighter than the A and B models that had preceded it and this allowed Suzuki to mount the engine lower in the frame. The resulting machine was easier on tyres and could change direction more quickly. It won the World Championship in the hands of Marco Lucchinelli while the title holders, Yamaha, were caught in a development year with a new square four that was

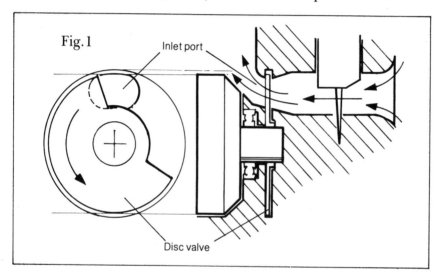

Fig. 1

Inlet port

Disc valve

The disc valve rotates across the inlet tract interrupting the gas flow.

a little large but necessary because their old engine was too slow.

Suzuki started the trend towards smaller, compact yet none the less powerful engines that everyone has followed. The legal limit of four cylinders restricts design freedom but there are many possible variations within the framework. Up until the amazing debut of Honda's NS500 V three two stroke at the Argentine GP in 1982 it looked as though a four cylinder disc valve[3] engine was essential for success (fig. 1). The non-disc valve, piston ported[4] engine relies on

3   A thin round disc normally mounted on the crank shaft at right angles to the axis of rotation. The engine's inlet tract passes through the disc which has an aperture cut in it. Only when the aperture in the disc uncovers the inlet tract can gasses pass into the engine. The disc controls the induction to occur at the designed time and prevents charge that has been sucked into the engine from being pushed back out when the piston descends.

4   Piston porting is the covering and uncovering of the ports or windows in the two stroke's cylinders by the motion of the piston. The inlet port in the base of the cylinder wall is uncovered as the piston rises and the charge is sucked in. The piston only covers the port after the piston has already fallen some distance and the pressure in the crank case can cause the charge to escape.

pressure waves reverberating in the inlet tract to limit the loss of charge back out of the carburettor.

Pressure waves are generated by sudden changes of pressure in the crankcases as the piston cuts across the port where the inlet tract opens into the cylinder at the top of the crankcases. The pressure shock wave travels at the speed of sound along the inlet tract from the engine to the carburettor. When the shock wave reaches the mouth of the carb it is reflected by the atmosphere and runs back into the engine. If the inlet tract, including the carb, is the correct length then the pressure wave will return to the crankcase at the same time as the charge is in danger of being pushed out by the descending piston.

The problem is that the length of the inlet tract is fixed and as the speed of sound is a constant then the time that the shock wave takes to make its trip up and down the tract is fixed by the design. This means that the shock wave reflection is only a help at a certain engine speed because the time it takes the piston to rise and fall varies with the rpm. The induced charge is less likely to be pushed out at high rpm because of the greater inertia of the speeding gas. By using the reflected wave and the inertia of the gas the two stroke racing engine can work well at high rpm and Yamaha have won eleven and Aermacchi/Harley-Davidson four World Championships in recent years proving that in the 250, 350 and 500 classes the piston ported engine is a powerful weapon.

Lack of flexibility has always been a problem with powerful piston ported engines and Yamaha have tried two different methods of improving the spread of power. These two methods, reed valves and variable geometry exhaust ports, are not unique to Yamaha but they in particular have had a good deal of success with both.

The reed valve[5] prevents the charge that has been sucked into the crankcases from escaping and this allows the use of large inlet ports without making the engine very inefficient at low engine speeds. The reed valve does have the disadvantage that the effort of opening the reeds does detract from the gas flow and this can cut the maximum power available. The 750 Yamaha which, thanks to its capacity had plenty of power, used reed valves very successfully to broaden the spread making the machine relatively easy to ride.

Dale Singleton, after two Daytona wins on his 750 Yamaha, not surprisingly rates the engine pretty highly: "It is probably one of the best racing motor cycles ever sold and if Yamaha had kept

5   A one way valving system that is sucked open by the crank case depression allowing the charge to flow in and then springs shut to prevent reverse flow. The valve consists of a cage containing a number of light petals or reeds made from plastic or steel which bend to open and close on demand.

The all-conquering 1981 Suzuki RG500 Gamma engine. Evidence of the recessed clutch can be seen by the actuating arm sunk into the gearbox cover.

developing it still would be. The engine gives good power and it's predictably reliable. The trouble is now that the 500 Suzukis produce more useable bottom end power and the Yamaha has fallen behind in engine and frame development."

Even before the 750 Yamaha first appeared in '74 as a 700, the company had had considerable success with a reed valve 500 which won the first Grand Prix it entered, the French at Paul Ricard in April '73. Jarno Saarinen rode the Yamaha four, code number OW20, and beat Phil Read on the works MV. Jarno was killed in the 350 race at Monza and that ended the year for the works Yamaha team but they ran the 500 again in '75 and Giacomo Agostini won the title. In '76 and '77 Suzuki dominated the 500 class with their disc valve fours and Yamaha concentrated on road bike development.

They returned in '77 with a completely new engine for Steve Baker and Johnny Cecotto. It had a bore and stroke of 56mm × 50.6mm and no reed valves. They had to make these changes in an attempt to match the power of the Suzuki. The removal of the reed valves smoothed the flow through the carbs and inlet tract at the expense of engine flexibility. The bore and stroke ratio was changed from the square 54 × 54mm to oversquare so that the revs could be increased without greatly increasing the mean piston speed.[6]

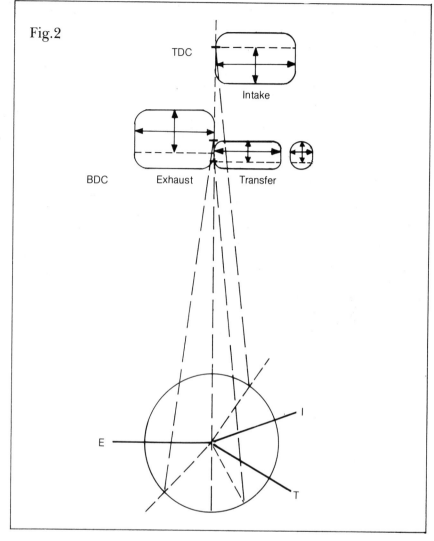

Fig.2

Although shortening the stroke reduces the port height, the increase in bore almost maintains the important port area which obviously affects the amount of fuel and air mixture that can flow through the engine. Porting is not as simple as that though because it is not only the physical area of the port that controls its size as far as the gasses are concerned. The time that the port spends open is as important as the area and so you will hear engine designers and tuners talk in terms of time-area which takes account both of the size of the port and the length of time it is uncovered by the piston (fig.2).

Time-area is quite a complicated thing to calculate because the

6   This is a measure of the stress imposed on the piston. Inertia stresses increase with the square of the speed so a small increase in piston speed can create a considerable increase in stress and a comparable loss in reliability.

The disc valve OW54 that Yamaha produced in a hurry for the beginning of the 1981 season when they realised that their piston ported machines could no longer be made competitive. By the time the 1982 OW60 had been produced the engine was much more compact, with the cylinders lying further forward, the water pump moved under the crankcases and the water pipes between the cylinders no longer showing.

piston is never moving at a steady speed as it runs up and down the bore. It is momentarily stationary at each end accelerating to maximum speed somewhere above the centre of the stroke and then slowing to a stop again. The piston speed varies because of the connection between it and the circular path of the crank pin to which it is tied by the con rod. The crank, of course, rotates at a constant speed at a given rpm. The varying piston speed means that the time-area of a port varies if you move its position up or down the bore.

Another consideration according to some designers is the speed of opening and closing of the port as it alters the Kadenacy effect[7]; in theory a stronger shock wave is created by the more sudden opening and closing. To make the wave stronger therefore some designers aim for a very square port with straight tops and bottoms. This gives a rapid opening and closing with the largest area for a given space but can be very hard on the piston ring[8] which tends to bulge out into a port as the piston passes. If the top or bottom edge of the port is horizontal then the ring may snag as it is forced out of the port and back into its groove in the piston.

Designers who believe this problem to be significant often use oval ports or at least curved rather than straight edges to ease the rings back into position. Tuners who have to make the best from large square ports will put a minute chamfer on the edge of the port to ease the passage of the ring. There is a trend towards having a greater number of smaller ports and this obviously greatly reduces the tendency of the ring to bulge. Protecting the ring is very important because not only will leakage reduce the power production but burning gasses that pass the ring will destroy the lubricating film of oil on the side of the piston.

There are two types of piston rings common in modern racing two strokes: plain rings and Dykes rings. The first has a straightforward, rectangular cross section and is used by Yamaha and Kawasaki. Suzuki prefer Dykes rings and Toni Mang used them in his own special 250 and 350 Kawasakis. The Dykes ring, originally invented by Paul de K. Dykes, has an L-shaped section and uses the considerable combustion pressure to help the lesser spring pressure hold the ring against the side of the cylinder, (fig.3). Both types of ring are prone to damage by badly designed ports.

7   The creation of a shock wave by the sudden opening or closing of a port.
8   Normally only one in the modern racing two stroke, this ring of alloy steel or iron is positioned in a groove in the piston near the head or crown, It is not a complete circle but has a break in it and is sprung so that it is always forcing itself outwards against the cylinder wall. It helps seal the piston, keeping the combustion gasses above the ring.

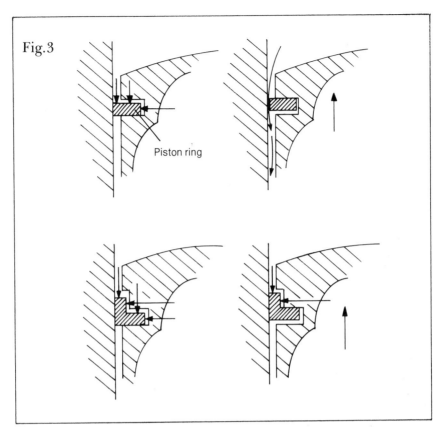

Fig.3

Piston ring

The L-shaped Dykes ring has the advantage of using the combustion gas pressure to force it against the cylinder wall.

All these considerations of port shapes and sizes must be taken into account by all two stroke engine designers as they were by Yamaha when they produced the OW35 for 1977 with the 56mm × 50.6mm bore and stroke. Neither Baker nor Cecotto shone on the machines but the following year Kenny Roberts used it to tremendous effect and won the World Championship against the established strength of Barry Sheene and the disc valve Suzuki. To help him succeed Yamaha did something to cure the inflexible engine that had hindered the team in '77.

They designed a variable geometry exhaust port. In search of more power to combat the Suzukis, Yamaha had consistently raised the exhaust port which gives more power at high revs. The high exhaust port makes the engine work poorly at slower rpm so in designing a variable port roof that was lowered at lower engine speeds it hence spreads the engine's power band. The lowering of the port roof was accomplished by an aluminium cylinder lying across the exhaust tract. The cylinder was almost completely machined away to allow the exhaust gasses to flow past but one section remained and when the cylinder was rotated about 12 degrees the segment of the cylinder would turn into the exhaust tract effectively lowering the port roof about four mm.

The cylindrical exhaust valve, or power valve as it became known, has been used on production racing 500 and 250 Yamahas. The works Yamahas have always used small, electric motors to open and close the valves controlled by electronics that read the engine revs. The production machines have used cheaper, mechanical, centrifugal devices to advance and retard the valves.

As a further refinement the machine that Roberts used to win the title in 1980 had a guillotine exhaust valve instead of the cylinder. This guillotine can be placed nearer to the piston than the cylinder, it is about 10mm (0.4in) wide and is controlled by a rack and pinion which in turn is powered by the electric motor. Although the guillotine version of the valve once tried was retained there was apparently little difference in performance. Surprisingly, although the cylindrical exhaust valve is some way from the piston and therefore there is certainly no seal between the piston ring and the cylinder it still has the effect of lowering the port height. This is not only true when the engine is turning over: the exhaust port in the lowered position so increases the compression that the engine cannot be started unless the valve is propped open.

The exhaust valve was enough to stave off the Suzuki attack until '81 when Marco Lucchinelli overwhelmed everyone with the way he rode the RG500 Gamma. It is surprising that Roberts managed to do what he did with the Yamaha because the exhaust valve could in no way match the flexible power output of the Suzuki. The disc valve indication system allows long inlet port opening without losing the charge back through the carbs and also more transfer ports[9] can be built into the cylinder which no longer contains an inlet port. The greater transfer port area obviously allows more gas to flow and more power to be made.

Harald Bartol, the notable Austrian engineer who has considerable experience of both the Morbidelli 125 disc valve twin and the works RG500 Suzuki as well as designing and building his own 250 and 350 disc valve twin, has firm ideas about that type of engine: "A disc valve engine has to be superior to a piston-ported design because of the asymetrical timing[10] but the actual timing of the disc is not critical to within one or two degrees."

The valve may open early but the gasses will only be sucked into the engine when the rise of the piston has created a depression or

9 The ports in the cylinder wall through which the incoming charge passes. Transfer passages are cast in the cylinder walls leading from the crankcases to the cylinder and the ports are uncovered by the piston at the bottom of its stroke.
10 Unlike the piston ported engine the disc valver does not have the inlet port open for the same period before the bottom of the piston stroke as it does after. See porting diagram 87.

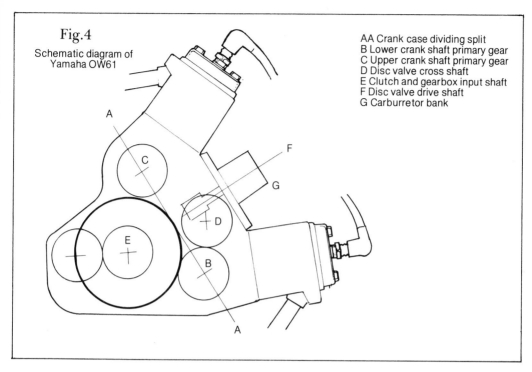

Fig.4

Schematic diagram of
Yamaha OW61

AA Crank case dividing split
B Lower crank shaft primary gear
C Upper crank shaft primary gear
D Disc valve cross shaft
E Clutch and gearbox input shaft
F Disc valve drive shaft
G Carburretor bank

the shock wave in the inlet tract draws them in. The trend is towards shorter and shorter carbs so that the short inlet tract makes the supercharging[11] effect of the pressure shock wave work at high rpm. So inlet timings tend to err on the early side.

The closing of the port by the disc may well be timed to occur after the piston has begun to fall because although the piston will be starting to pressurize the crankcase, the inertia of the incoming gas will carry it in for some time after the crankcase pressure has passed atmospheric pressure. Altering disc timings will affect engine performance but generally not within a few degrees. What is important is that the port be closed by the time the crankcase gasses want to escape. The disc does have the added advantage of being good for the Kadenacy effect and creates a very strong pressure wave.

The Suzuki works RG500s have gone through two major changes to make the engine more compact. The first engine, the RGA, was a pure square four with two banks of cylinders leaning a few degrees forward. The drive was taken from the four cranks by a central gear which passed it to another idler gear and from there to the clutch. The A model won Sheene two World Championships but the B was smaller, thanks to the disappearance of the idler gear.

A schematic diagram of Yamaha's OW61 V four showing the layout of the cylinders cylinder, disc valves and shafts. In 1984 the OW76 replaced this engine. It had a similar layout but with reed valves replacing the discs and breathing direct into the crank cases.

11 Supercharging refers to forced induction normally using a mechanical pump, or super-charger. It also describes forced induction by pressure waves.

This was done by stepping the cylinders, moving the rear bank up and the front pair back so that the primary gear and shaft that took the drive from the cranks could inpart it to the clutch. Such engines are much more expensive to produce as the shafts are no longer all on the same crankcase split. The loss of a gear and shaft reduces friction, saving power. A later modification of the B was the design of the quickly removable gear cluster. This idea was also adopted by Yamaha. By removing the clutch, access is gained to the gearbox cover plate. Remove this and with it comes the gear cluster without the need to split the engine which is more normal. By being able to change the internal ratio quickly riders have a chance of selecting exactly the right gear for a particularly important corner. Teams may have as many as four or five possible ratios for each of the six gears and being able to change them quickly is vital in the limited practice time available.

The third, Gamma, version of the RG was the result of a meeting between the works riders Randy Mamola and Graeme Crosby and the design engineers in Japan at the end of the 1980 season. Crosby later explained what they had asked for: "We drew a list of things on the black board: we asked that it be made smaller, lower, lighter and if possible with more power. But really it was just about quick enough already." The riders got what they wanted because the Gamma was a masterpiece of conservative redesign, certainly smaller and lighter, it was faster perhaps because of that rather than any great increase in power.

The cranks were strengthened and made smaller by putting the pairs of cylinders on single cranks with a single central primary drive gear for each pair. The discs and covers were recessed into the crankcases which both reduced the engine width and the inlet tract length. The clutch was also sunk into the gearbox side cover and all this meant that the engine could be mounted lower in the frame without it grounding during cornering.

When Kawasaki decided to contest the 500 class they built a square four which broadly speaking uses the same engine layout as the Suzuki although the banks of cylinders are not stepped but lean forward. Yamaha realised that they could not stretch their piston ported four any further and they too built a similar disc valve square four, retaining their guillotine exhaust valves. After riding piston ported Yamahas all his road racing life, Kenny Roberts found the tractable power of the disc valve engine a revelation: "Before I rode the disc valver I'd never ridden a road racer with four stroke power. It comes in so low you can spin the back tyre at almost any speed. In 1982 I was using that low down power to turn the bike going on to the banking at Daytona, I was coming out of the infield heading for the wall and turning the bike by sliding the back end. At higher revs, between 12 and 13,000, the old piston ported bike really carried its weight well, perhaps better than the rotary valve but as a racing engine the new one is much more useable." The fact that the three opposition factories all had disc valve fours may have influenced Honda's decision to build a reed valve three when they entered racing at the beginning of '82 but this was not a major consideration according to Miokoshi, who leads the team of designers: "I have had a lot of experience with motocross engines and I can remember testing the first 250 twin cylinder engines in comparison with our 250 single and finding that the twin produced less power because of the internal friction both in the crank shaft bearings etc. and the pistons. The NS500 has a single crank shaft to reduce to the absolute minimum the internal friction and three cylinders are sufficient for the power we need because we have a low weight and small frontal area." (See chapter 2.) "I do not know what the four cylinder machines are producing but I doubt it is more than 130bhp and we already have 125bhp from our three. Our motocross development has also produced some very advanced reed valves that open by detracting very little from the energy of the gas stream and the layout will not allow us to use disc valves."

Miokoshi had few words to say in praise of the NR500 four stroke project: "Although our company would like to win a Grand Prix with a four stroke and may do so in the future, the NR500 has not achieved the goals set for it. Our success depends on the two stroke."

It was obvious from first glance that the NS500 Honda is a very compact engine with two cylinders leaning a few degrees forward of vertical and the third cylinder pointing down and forward in a 110 degree V with the others. The three carbs nestle in the V with their bores horizontal. The three pistons are all connected to the same crankshaft. The left hand end of the crank drives the water pump and the right hand end the total loss, battery-powered ignition system. The 62.6mm bore × 54mm stroke makes a capacity of 498.6cc but when the bike made its debut at the Argentine GP it was surprising to see that the expansion chambers[12] had been flattened and twisted to fit the available space.

This means that the expansion chambers cannot operate as efficiently as perfectly straight round section pipes. Experience suggests that a badly deformed chamber like the one that passes under the engine from the forward cylinder might lose 3bhp. It is both surprising that Honda thought they could afford to lose

horsepower through each of the three cylinders and also that the machine still seemed to be reasonably competitive. The two rearward facing pipes crossed over under the seat so that the silencers[13] did not extend beyond the rear tyre.

The rearward facing expansion chambers hidden beneath the seat were pressed in two halves and welded along the seams. This pressed construction allows very complex smooth curves to be produced. Completely seamless pipes may be produced by using hydraulic pressure to blow tubing into a shaped mould but still by far the most usual method is to weld the pipe together from many

12 Two stroke exhaust pipes are referred to as expansion chambers because the bulbous nature of the pipe draws the exhaust gasses out of the cylinder. The sides of the pipe diverge as it leaves the cylinder. The gasses leave the cylinder at a speed determined by the pressure of the trapped gasses. The inertia of the gas tries to maintain the same speed down the pipe but the diameter of the pipe grows forcing more gas out of the cylinder. This inertia effect is aided by the high pressure shock waves leaving the cylinder. These are turned around by the diverging walls and run back to the cylinder as low pressure waves adding to the vacuum. This has the effect of clearing the cylinder more efficiently of the burnt gasses and also helps draw the fresh charge up the transfer ports and into the cylinder in time for the next compression stroke. If the pipe continued to expand a lot of the fresh charge that rushes into the cylinder through the transfer ports would flow straight out of the exhaust pipe before it could be trapped by the rising piston shutting

conical sections.

The shape of the expansion chamber can become very complex as the designer aims for maximum power output. The diverging, or diffuser, cone in its simplest form will have a taper of about 8 degrees. A wider taper can produce more power but over a smaller rev range; a narrower taper may afford a better spread but less power. If in search for more power a wider taper is considered, the flow of gas will not remain in contact with the sides of the exhaust and the turbulence will destroy the power producing suction. It has been found that a narrow taper is needed at first near the cylinder

off the exhaust port. To prevent this the tail section of the exhaust pipe has a converging cone that bounces a pressure wave back to help push the fresh charge back into the cylinder effectively closing the port early. The pressure wave is created due to the Kadenacy effect page 90. And just like the inlet tract length, the length of the exhaust pipe is critical and is only effective over a small rev change. After the converging cone a small diameter tail pipe lets the gasses out into the atmosphere. The tail pipe can be of small diameter because the exhaust can pass through during the entire crank rotation.

13 All racing machines must be silenced (chapter 3 page 74) and almost invariably the absorption silencer is used. This places no obstruction in the tail pipe but the sound waves are absorbed through a metal mesh into glass or asbestos fibre contained in a cannister on the end of the exhaust pipe.

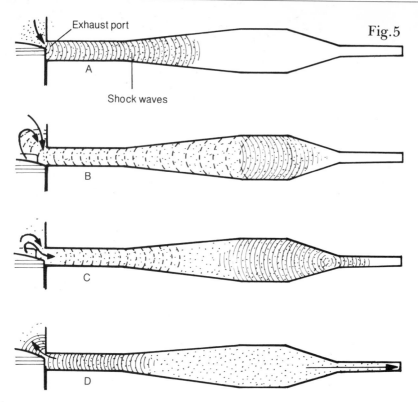

Exhaust port

Fig.5

Shock waves

A

B

C

D

where the gas speed is highest but the angle can increase as the gas speed slows. This leads designers to aim for a trumpet shape with either cones of several different angles or a pressing with a gradual change. Designers aiming for greater torque and low speed power production have an almost parallel section of pipe leading from the cylinder to the first diffuser but high performance racing engines have only a very short section in search of greater peak power.

The shape and positioning of the reverse cone is calculated from the speed of sound in the pipe and the rev range in which the engine is designed to operate. If the reverse cone was in fact replaced with a flat plate it would obviously reflect a very strong wave but as the speed of sound is constant the wave would only be rebounded at the correct time for one specified rpm. A cone spreads the effect over a reasonable rev range. To position the cone one must of course know what the spread of sound is in the chamber, for that is the speed of the shock wave. The speed of sound varies with air temperature and pressure and they both vary along the exhaust pipe. Leaving the cylinder the gas temperature is about 700 °C (1,300 °F) but as the gas expands it cools to about 250 °C (480 °F) before being compressed and heated again to about 450 °C (840 °F) at the tail pipe. So calculating the air temperature and pressure and hence the speed of sound you should use

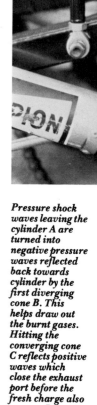

Pressure shock waves leaving the cylinder A are turned into negative pressure waves reflected back towards cylinder by the first diverging cone B. This helps draw out the burnt gases. Hitting the converging cone C reflects positive waves which close the exhaust port before the fresh charge also escapes D.

becomes very difficult unless you have a great deal of data on expansion chambers known to be effective in which case you can work from there. The speed turns out to be about 1,640 ft/sec (500m/sec) but even the best designers will accept a degree of trial and error.

Although the 500cc class belongs to the major manufacturers, wealthy sponsors like Pernod can afford to produce machines such as the disc valve, water-cooled twin.

You will often see expansion chambers wrapped with asbestos especially over the first part of their length. This can be done for several reasons. One may be an attempt to raise the temperature of the air in the chamber which will in turn raise the speed of the reflected wave. A wave that returns quicker will be effective at a higher engine speed and hence wrapping the pipe may move the rev range a few hundred revs higher. Another reason may be to damp out the vibration of the steel expansion chamber itself as this can cause the metal to harden and fracture. Expansion chambers are never bolted to the cylinder but are held on by springs so that they have a small degree of vibration isolation.

Flat-sided expansion chambers are much more prone to 'ring' with vibration than those of round section and are more likely to fracture as well as producing more noise and less power. Interruptions and diversions away from the ideal conical sections have a worse effect on the exhaust pipes' pressure wave propogation and power production than well designed changes of will turn along it without much problem but a dented, kinked or flattened pipe will have shock waves ricochetting around inside very much to the detriment of power production.

Honda developed their own system of exhaust control to give their machines more flexibility and called it ATAC meaning Automatic Torque Amplification Control. The system employs a small box added to the side of the pipe just after it leaves the cylinder. Opening a valve between the pipe and the chamber at low revs raises the volume of the expansion chamber making it work at lower revs. The valve is closed mechanically as engine revs increase and the gasses are left to run straight through to a lower volume high revving pipe. Honda employed this system on the later NS500 works machines, the 1985 RS500 production racer and the NSR500 V four works bike.

Between the induction system, that is instrumental in controlling the fresh charge of air and fuel on its way into the engine, and the exhaust pipe, that draws and organises its expulsion, is the piston and combustion chamber where the power is produced. The combustion chamber with its ports through which the gasses flow and the piston crown and cylinder head which when forced together form the tiny space for initial burning is the works teams' most jealously guarded secret. You can take photographs of expansion chambers and scale out the dimensions and similarly you might work out the induction length but what goes on inside the cylinder castings will remain a secret for as long as the works team manager desires.

The general principles are well known enough: the gasses are forced up the transfer ports and into the cylinder, the flow directed by the angle of the ducts. Virtually all high performance two strokes work on a loop scavenge[14] system attributed to Dr. Schneurle. It is called loop scavenging because the gasses loop up around the back and top of the cylinder before going out of the exhaust port (fig.6).

The shape and angle of the ports dictate the direction of flow and it is the fresh charge that expunges the last remnants of burnt gasses from the previous cycle. The better the scavenge system the less burnt gas will remain in the cylinder to foul the fresh charge. The transfer ports are directed towards the back of the cylinder, away from the exhaust port. In the case of the disc valve engines that have no inlet port in their rear walls there is room for another transfer port which obviously affects the flow pattern. The situation is so complex and difficult to analyse that a mixture of

14 The process by which the burnt gasses are removed from the cylinder and replaced by fresh.

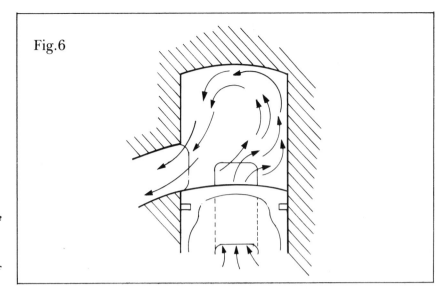

Fig.6

A loop scavenge system uses shaped transfer ports to direct the incoming charge up towards the rear of the cylinder. This sweeps it clear of burnt gases.

science and experience is required. Even those masters of the art, like Jorg Muller, Harald Bartol, Jan Thiel and Martin Mijwaart who must have designed, cast and finely tuned hundreds of two stroke barrels on machines from 50cc to 750cc, do not have anywhere near all the answers. Dr. Gordon Blair has spent many years at the Queen's University, Belfast, using a computer to predict the result of changes to two stroke internals. He has done a great deal of work in association with Yamaha and several Japanese engineers have produced very informative SAE[15] papers on specific aspects of two stroke engines. There is enough to fill many large volumes on two stroke racing engine design. The most difficult thing is to separate fact from fiction, science from folklore. One of the problems is that when a tuner succeeds in producing a power increase from his engine he may not be certain as to what created the gain, it is easy to be misled. There are many subjects on which knowledgeable people disagree: should the crankcase volume be kept to a minimum to give a maximum primary compression ratio to pump gasses into the cylinder or does this restrict the amount of fuel and air drawn into the crank case in the first place? Should the piston and head be machined to create a very wide squish band[16] or does that create too high a compression ratio and give the gas too little chance of escape from the squish area? Should the combustion chamber not be central but moved towards the back of the cylinder away from the exhaust port? The

15 Society of Automotive Engineers, Inc., 400 Commonwealth Drive, Warrendale, PA 15096, USA. Publishers of scientific papers on all subjects.

16 Squish areas are created where the piston at the top of its stroke comes so close to the piston [within 0.040 in (1.016mm)] that virtually all the gas is squirted out into the desired combustion chamber. In a two stroke the squish band is created around the edge of the piston and across about half its width.

The NS500 surprised everyone by being nearly as fast as a four cylinder, disc valve machine.

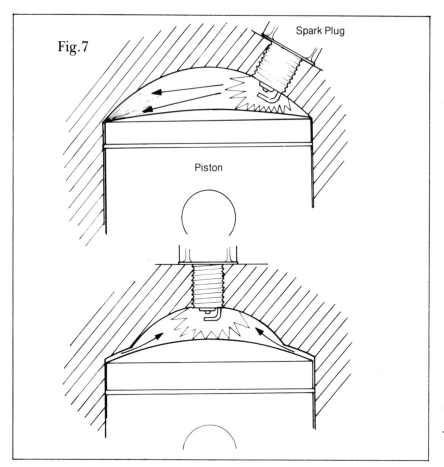

Fig.7

Spark Plug

Piston

By using a squish area gases are forced into a more compact combustion chamber.

piston is most prone to overheating near the exhaust port because the back of the piston is cooled by the fresh incoming charge. Many manufacturers including Yamaha have tried aiming the heat of the combustion chamber towards the rear of the cylinder away from the exhaust port in an attempt to even up the thermal load on the piston and thus enable them to run a higher compression ratio[17] and hence get more power without suffering detonation. Detonation occurs when the combination of temperature and compression causes the fuel and air to explode before being triggered by the spark. This reduces power and will eat away at the piston and head eventually holing the piston. Low octane fuel detonates more readily and therefore requires a lower compression ratio.

17 This is the ratio the volume of the gasses collected in the cylinder after induction to the volume at the top of the piston's stroke when combustion occurs. In a four stroke it is simple to calculate the volume at the bottom of the piston's stroke but because a two stroke only traps its charge when all the ports are closed by the piston the question is more complex. Real two stroke compression ratios are lower than the numerical value calculated in the same way as the four stroke but higher than that calculated from the closing of the exhaust port thanks to the expansion chamber's pressurizing effect.

Most designers have reverted to central spark plugs in hemispherical combustion chambers because they offer the best compromise of thermal loading on the piston and excellent gas burning. The heat of combustion is transferred to the piston mainly through the area under the combustion chamber and hence the squish band shields a proportion of the piston from the initial heat of the flame. As heat absorption is proportional to area there is good reason to have a large squish band to keep the heat absorbed by the piston to a minimum (fig. 7).

It is the piston that is the weakest point as far as the two stroke's power production is concerned. It is the piston that seizes if it overheats or gets holed through detonation. The piston is made from aluminium with a high, 15% to 25%, silicon[18] content. This reduces the aluminium's expansion rate and greatly improves its hot strength.

Racing pistons are forged[19] rather than cast[20] because the act of forging works the crystalline structure into the correct alignment for maximum strength.

The piston only has two ways of dissipating the heat it is subjected to by the combustion: to the cool fresh charge below it in the crankcase and above it as the charge enters the cylinder, and by conduction to the water-cooled cylinder walls. The relationship between the piston, the cylinder wall and the oil film that lubricates the pair is critical. The oil is carried mixed in the petrol and is spread around the bearings and cylinder by the fuel mist. The piston must expand against the cylinder wall at running temperature if it is to help the piston ring seal and pass on its heat to the cylinder. It must not come into plain metal-to-metal contact or the aluminium will weld itself to the wall causing a seizure.

The oil is designed to cling to the metal and will not be pushed aside no matter how hard the piston forces against the cylinder unless the temperature reaches the charring point of the oil at which point its lubrication properties are destroyed. Temperature is obviously very important and often mechanics will study the top of the piston to tell by the colour of combustion the temperature of the piston. A truer indication, but more difficult to see, is underneath the piston crown where the lubricating oil will be painted a shiny black. It is when the oil that has hardened like lacquer becomes matt from charring that the oil has exceeded its lubricating temperature and failure is just around the corner.

Pistons are cheaper to replace than cylinders and the cylinders

18 A non metallic element, symbol Si. Silicon is the second most abundant element.
19 Formed from a solid billet or lump by stamping into shape by a series of formed tools.
20 Molten metal is poured into a mould of the desired shape.

are protected by a coating of particularly hard material such as Nicasil or chromium electro plating[21] or, in the case of Kawasaki, an electro fusion coating. They run a thin wire up the centre of the bore and then pass a large current through it. Much like a fuse blowing, the wire explodes depositing globules of molten metal on the surface of the aluminium casting. This process is repeated to produce the required layer. None of these coatings look like glossy chrome plating because they need a matt finish to help retain the oil film.

21 Electro plating is a process by which the metal object to be plated is immersed in a fluid containing dissolved metal salts. An electric current is passed through the fluid via the metal object. Certain metal salts will migrate to the object as they pass the current and deposit themselves on the surface. Chrome plating is common but Nicasil, a combination of nickel and silicon is tougher, more wear resistant.

Water cooling is now deemed essential for racing engines and most designers concern themselves with maintaining a running temperature around 158°F (70°C) though Harald Bartol prefers to run his engines at between 60° and 70°C. "I have found that engines produce their best power closer to 60°C and it drops off quickly above 70°." Although overheating will cause a loss in power, and above 90°C the piston may well seize, there is also the risk, especially in cold weather in England, of cold seizures. This occurs when the piston does not expand properly to create the correct running fit in the bore. The piston does not seal and the ring alone cannot stop the combustion gasses from blowing down the side of the piston and burning away the lubricating film.

Although similar in layout to the 250 Rotax, the Barry Hart designed Armstrong 350 engine (fitted here to the Armstrong carbon fibre frame) has a horizontally split crank case and proved very competitive in its class.

Without the oil the piston rubs on the cylinder and seizes. This explains why warming up the engine before racing is important: it must come up to the correct working temperature before being stressed under load. Part of the radiator will be taped over in cold weather.

The next most vulnerable part of the engine after the piston are the bearings of the connecting rod and the crankshaft. Bearings are either ball or roller depending on the space available and the loads they have to withstand. The small diameter roller bearings, or needle rollers, are used in the small end[22] bearing as there is little space and it is important to keep the reciprocating weight[23] to a minimum. Roller bearings can withstand a greater load than ball bearings because of the greater linear contact compared with the

22 The small end of the connecting rod is the end connected to the piston. It is a smaller diameter than the big end connected to the crank shaft.
23 A weight that moves backwards and forwards and therefore has to be constantly accelerated and decelerated.

Using much of the experience they gained through winning World championships with their KR250, Kawasaki produced a disc valve, square four 500 which has a similar lay-out to the Suzuki and Yamaha square fours.

For 20 years Yamaha have produced production racers for the privateer. The power valve TZ250 proved to be nearly as fast as the disc valve opposition.

ball's point contact.

Ball bearings absorb less power than roller bearings so the temptation is to use ball races and replace them more frequently. The life of a bearing is dependent both on the loads imposed on it and the number of times the load is applied and released, or cycled. Increase the rpm limit, which means that the increased piston speed greatly increases the load in the bearings both of the con rod and the crankshaft, and the bearings will fail in fewer engine rotations. Experience with an engine tells the engineer the length of service that can be expected from the bearings before they should be replaced prior to failure. Of course bearings sometimes fail early; this can be because of over revving, a foreign particle in the bearing, poor quality of material or heat treatment, or misalignment of the bearing itself or the crankshaft. Suzuki Italy team manager Roberto Gallina has had plenty of experience with the works RG500 engines that lead him to the conclusion that if the

Alain Chevallier tends to a TZ250 Yamaha engine which he is about to test on his dynamometer.

Suzuki's RG500 Mark VI was a typical square four design. The crankshafts lie parallel with a primary drive gear in the centre of each bank. Underneath and in between these two primary gears is another gear on the end of a jack shaft which drives the clutch from its other end. The pistons and con rods lying loose in this dismantled engine run in cylinders vertical to the crankshafts.

crankshaft assembly lasted a running in period it would not fail over a Grand Prix distance. He used that fact during 1981 as his rider Marco Lucchinelli swept to the 500cc world title: "We built two new engines for practice and decided early on which engine was the fastest and that one would be the race engine. That engine we would run for between 100km and 160km (60 and 100 miles) and then the night before the race strip that engine completely. If the bearings showed no sign of blueing, indicating over heating, then they were virtually certain to run a Grand Prix without trouble."

There is no doubt that designing and building racing engines is an exact science. Alignment of crankshafts and their bearing housings in the crankcases are crucial to performance and reliability. Mechanics will spend many hours building an engine to get it as close as possible to the designer's ideal, measuring combustion chamber volumes to match one cylinder to another, comparing con rod lengths to make sure they are all identical. The difference between an engine that is put together by a really skilled man and set up to perfection and an engine that has any selection of parts pulled down from the shelf can be 10% of the horsepower or the difference between running for 300 miles or 3.

One example is the selection of pistons. Yamaha's pistons for their 250 racers for example have always been marked with their sizes 96, 97, 98, 99. Referring to their actual size compared with the nominal 54mm bore, they mean the piston is 53.96 or 53.98 etc. and the barrels are also marked. .000 is perfectly 54.000mm but .014 is 54.014mm. You should match the correct pistons with the correct barrels to give the correct running clearance. But experienced mechanics know not to believe the manufacturers markings and will search through the parts box using a micrometer to select exactly the right sized pistons for their engines.

Just to confound anyone who might think that they understand what is required to make an engine a Grand Prix winner there are always stories that confound theory. Kork Ballington won both the 250 and 350 British Grands Prix in 1977 on his Yamahas but as his brother and mechanic Deryck remembers, the night before the race things looked bleak: "The 250 had been peppering its cylinder head with rivets from the main bearings and that was in pieces. The 350 had been detonating badly on one side and when I measured the con rods one was .3mm (.012in) longer than the other and that of course was the cylinder that was detonating. It had had about a third less clearance at the squish band but I didn't want to change the con rod because it was a good crank and was running true. All I could do was put the piston in the lathe and skim the head. It looked more like a cone on top when I had finished instead of a dome but it did cut down the compression."

Deryck's story about their first Grand Prix win, the Spanish in '76, is even more amazing and perfectly illustrates the plight of the privateer with no money to buy spare parts. "The 350 (Yamaha) had been detonating so badly on one side that the barrel had been eaten away through to the 'O' ring groove in one place. My grinding tools had been stolen so I had to use a file to reduce the compression in the head. Then I cut a lump of aluminium from the lug on the front of the barrel that holds the exhaust pipe springs. I filed that to fit the hole in the cylinder and tapped it in, leaving it standing a bit proud so that it was held in place by the cylinder head. It worked long enough for Kork to win the race but, thank God, I don't have to do that sort of thing any more."

The thing that makes Deryck, always known as Doze, the brilliant mechanic that he is, is that he must have a natural feel for what can be done in an emergency that stands a reasonable chance of lasting the distance and the reliability record of the works Kawasakis that he prepared for Kork to win the 250 and 350 titles in '78 and '79 was virtually unbeatable.

Although the major factories now spend almost all their money on the 500 class there is a great deal of skill and ingenuity in the smallest classes, 50cc and 80cc, as their protagonists like Ricardo Tormo are quick to point out: "It takes a lot of work to get one more horsepower from a 50cc or 80cc engine and if my engineer, Angel Carmona, can get one horsepower from my single then I'm sure he could get five or ten horsepower from a four cylinder 500."

5

Steering, suspension and frames

Motor cycle racing is far from merely being a contest of power alone. A fantastic engine is of little use to the rider if he cannot make use of its power because the wheels are not constantly in contact with the ground or are often pointing in a direction other than the intended course. The frame, steering and suspension must be so designed that the rider can turn the engine's power into speed around the circuit.

To keep the correct relationship between the engine and the front and rear suspension, the frame must have a certain strength and rigidity for minimum weight. The frame also has to support the rider and provide mounting points for the fairing, petrol tank and instruments. It is surprising but the motor cycle frame has remained little changed through many decades of development.

By far the majority of frames are cradles constructed in tubing with the engine sitting in the centre. The engine forms such a large part of the machine that there is little choice in the matter; the engine, being a rigid cast structure, contributes to the strength of the frame. Intelligent designers have always sought to make the greatest use of the engine as a stressed[1] member and several of today's racing machines would be in danger of collapsing if you sat on them with the engine removed.

Even using the engine well still leaves the motor cycle frame to do a good deal of work because no one has yet designed a power plant which is the right shape to hold the major components together on its own. Perhaps this shows a lack of co-ordination between engine and frame design teams but on the other hand such a structure might not be any lighter than current racing frames which for a 350 or 500 can weigh as little as 12 to 15 lbs (5.4 to 6.8 kg).

While some of the major Japanese manufacturers' design teams certainly use computers to construct mathematical models with which to improve their frame designs, it is interesting to note that individuals who rely on their own training, good sense and experience are still very often responsible for the best racing

1   Load bearing.

The first KR500, the 1980 version, used the petrol tank as the monocoque's main structural member and the engine helped with rigidity. Because it vibrated, rubber mounted handlebars were needed to isolate the rider.

frames. Honda had the foresight to employ the services of Ron Williams, whose own frames have won numerous Isle of Man TTs, to help them develop their racing machines including the NR and NS500s as well as the 1000cc four strokes.

His method of frame design is disarmingly simple when he is working alone on a new project. "I don't spend hours at the drawing board laying out every tube, but I spend a day or so drawing up the major points: the engine position, wheel centres, suspension etc."

"Then in my workshop in Cheshire I take an engine and position it in the frame which is adjustable so I can use it for all my bikes and then it is quite easy to lay the tubes around it. The engine position is very important, critical to the weight distribution which affects everything else. It is something that I have developed a feeling for. Many of todays engines are so large that they virtually dictate where you position the wheels and suspension etc. The relationship between the engine sprockets, the rear wheel sprockets and the swing arm pivot must also be carefully considered and by the time I have done that the wheel base may well be determined and I have found that it is not critical to within an inch or so."

As Ron points out, the engine does greatly influence frame design and as the trend is towards smaller and smaller machines in an attempt to reduce the frontal area and hence the aerodynamic

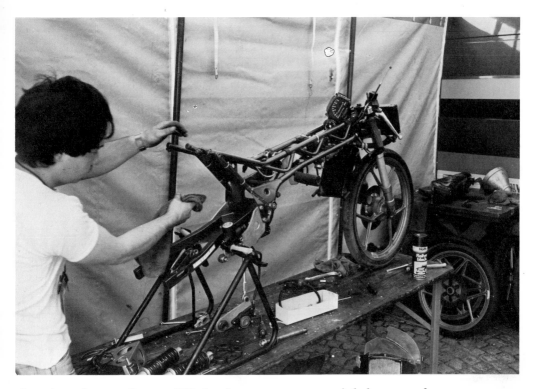

drag (see chapter 2 page 56) the frame must wrap tightly around the power plant. Virtually all racing machines use some sort of forks as front suspension and steering and these require a steering head.[2]

The 50cc Kreidler had a backbone structure using four main straight tubes with numerous connecting struts.

The steering head should be as long as possible to reduce the concentration of the tremendous braking and cornering stresses transmitted from the front forks. There is a major difference of opinion concerning the positioning of frame tubes around the steering head. While one school of thought considers that the tubes should be splayed wide so as to withstand the side forces or twisting imposed by cornering, the opposition, including Ron Williams, maintain that by far the greatest loads are incurred under braking and therefore the tubes must run straight back at a narrow angle. Because Ron Williams always stresses his frames to resist the tremendous loads incurred under heavy braking, he cringes when riders pull wheelies to show off then slam the front wheel back on the ground. This stresses the frame in exactly the opposite direction by tending to kick the front wheel forward.

There is a very important fact that adds weight to the second view: forces transmitted to the frame can be considered to originate from or at least be limited by the tyres and the friction developed at the contact patch (chapter 6). During cornering the

2 Normally a tube containing a bearing at each end in which the front forks can swivel.

115

weight of the machine is distributed between the two wheels and this limits the amount of friction that can be generated by either (page 145). Under braking however virtually the entire weight of the machine is thrown quite suddenly onto the front wheel and therefore the maximum friction is generated and the maximum force is transmitted.

Gregg Hansford wheelies the old 750cc Kawasaki at Laguna Seca.

The situation is more complex than that when you consider the point at which the rider starts to lean into the corner while still braking. But it remains true that as soon as some of the weight is transferred from the front wheel to the back (and this must occur before leaning or the back wheel will step sideways out of control) then the friction generated at the front wheel must be reduced.

The rigidity of the steering head can be improved by cross bracing between the frame tubes that run down to the front of the engine and this helps withstand cornering stresses. Braking stresses require designs with splayed tubes around the head to include substantial gusseting. Splaying the tubes does allow the designer to sink the petrol tank inside the frame and this can enable him to place the considerable weight of the fuel lower.

With the longest steering head possible the designer will then be looking to conduct the stress as close to the rear engine mountings and the swinging arm pivot as possible. In most middle and large capacity machines two triangles are constructed, side by side, over the top of the engine with the steering head as the single common side. A three sided figure is far more rigid than any other and frame tubes should always be laid out in triangles where possible. The larger the triangle the better as this will take the stress closest to the swing arm. Lone, untriangulated tubes must be kept as short as possible and should be avoided altogether. The frame tubes running down to the front of the engine intersect with the upper frame tubes and these are used to further reinforce the head area. The problem with building the ideal large triangles over the top of the engine is that this is likely to restrict access to the engine and may prevent removal of the cylinders. It is obviously no good having a superb frame if the mechanics cannot work on the engine and such considerations often limit frame design.

Once the steering head has been successfully joined to the engine the frame's most critical job is done. Although frames are often complete loops, with tubes running under the engine, these should be redundant as long as the engine mounting points are substantial enough for the engine to take the load.

What other demands are placed on the frame depends on the type of rear suspension used. While the suspension unit or units are connected at one end to the swing arm the other end must be

*Franco Uncini
served a long
apprenticeship
as a privateer
before he
received works
support.*

mounted in the frame and there may also be rockers to be pivoted in the frame. These load points are highly stressed though not quite as highly as the steering head. Many rear suspension designers require a rear sub-frame to be built over the back wheel and this normally doubles as a seat support. It makes sense to construct the sub-frame from two triangles.

The tubing used to construct racing frames comes from two groups of materials: aluminium alloys and steel alloys. The steel alloys, commonly Reynolds 531 and T45, have been used for many years. They offer excellent strength-for-weight characteristics and when treated correctly are resistant to cracking. It is important not to overheat the metal when it is being welded[3] or the structure of the metal will be altered and the strength destroyed to the point where cracking soon occurs.

Metals have a crystalline structure[4] and the size of the crystals and distribution of any non-homogenous[5] particles within it is greatly affected not only by the alloying elements present but heating and cooling that the metal has been subjected to. The subject of metallurgy is deep and complex and there is no point in going deeper into it here but suffice to say heat applied to all high performance alloys can have crucial effects.

To keep heat to a minimum it is usual not to weld steel alloys but to use brazing or bronze welding[6] which only requires the steel to be raised to 427°C (800°F) well below the 1400°C (2500°F) that is a typical melting point for steel.

Aluminium alloys are a different problem. They cannot be joined by anything other than aluminium and the alloys used in frame making must be arc welded[7] in a gas shroud to prevent oxidisation.[8]

Although weight for weight aluminium is not necessarily stronger than steel, current design trends use the fact that for the same weight you get a greater mass of aluminium and this can be used to employ larger sections which are inherently stiffer. Larger diameter tubing will always be stronger both against bending and twisting even though thinner wall thicknesses must be used for the

3 Welding is the joining of two suitable pieces of metal or plastic together by raising the temperature of thee mterial to the point where they melt and flow together.
4 On a microscopic level the molecules can be seen to be grouped together so that their boundaries form distinct plains. The size of the crystals, the orientation of the plains and any material interspersed between the crystals all effect the material properties.
5 A homogenous system is one where the chemical composition and physical state of any small proportion of the substance is the same as any other.
6 Brazing and bronze welding uses a brass based filler rod which is melted between the red hot steel parent metal. On solidification a strong joint is made.
7 Making a high voltage electric current jump between an electrode and the work piece, the metal is melted.
8 The growth of an aluminium oxide skin which melts at a very high temperature and prevents welding.

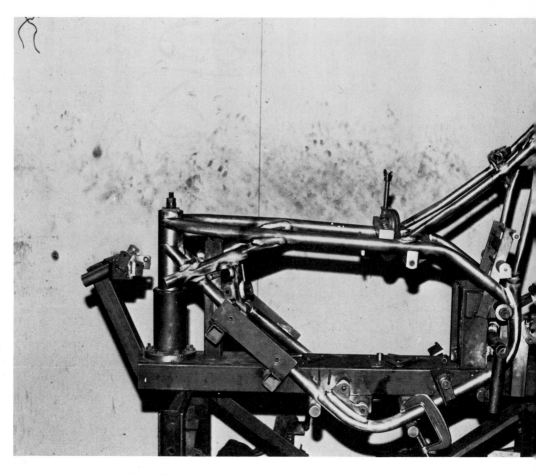

This Harris replica of a Yamaha frame has only a small triangle behind the steering head Their own designs have the stiffer, larger triangle which shortens the unsupported length of tube running over the engine to the swinging arm pivot. The picture shows the frame under construction in a jig which is required to maintain all the critical dimensions while the frame is being bronze welded together.

section of tubing to weigh the same. It becomes impractical to use very thin, very large cross section steel tubing because the paper thin walls could not stand knocks by a mechanic's hammer, stones thrown up from the road or the location of engine, or even fairing, mounting brackets. For the same weight one is able to have a thicker walled aluminium tube of the same diameter.

One design possibility is to take the giant, thin walled tube logic to its limit and build a spine frame or even a monocoque.[9] Spine frames enjoyed a vogue some years ago and used a single, very large diameter tube to join the steering head to the swinging arm pivot as directly as possible with no triangulation. The spine frame relies on single tubes of a large diameter to provide all the resistance to both twisting and bending. This it can do but spine frames tend to have no easy provision for engine mountings, tank, seat, suspension and fairing mountings. By the time these are added any weight advantage that a single tube had is almost

9 As the dictionary defines it, a monocoque is a body in which all structural loads are born by the skin.

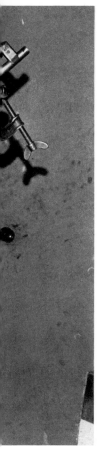

A strong
connection
between the
steering head
and the frame
tubes is essential.
The tube ends
have been
fashioned so that
they fit the
steering head
perfectly and a
minimum of
bronze filler will
be used to make
the joint.

certainly lost.

A monocoque ideally would be a box, suitably shaped to perform all the tasks not covered by the engine and the steering and suspension systems. In a Formula One racing car it does just that, acting in some cases as part of the streamlining as well as being the fuel tank and providing a cockpit for the driver. Several attempts have been made to do similar things in the motor cycle world without anyone having sufficient significant or lasting success to convince the majority of designers to follow suit. The first problem with a motor cycle is that to use the monocoque as streamlining, one would have to encase the engine. Honda made a brave attempt to do this with their original NR500 but two major stumbling blocks caused them to discard the idea. It made the mechanics' life almost impossible. To do anything at all to the engines they had to be removed from the enclosing monocoque. To keep the weight of the design down, thin gauge aluminium alloy was used and it could not withstand high frequency vibrations. Severe cracking was common and the monocoque was soon replaced by a conventional, tubular steel cradle.

A more common monocoque system is one which employs the petrol tank as a major structural member. Such monocoques have been made from cast magnesium but a more common method is to use welded box sections of sheet aluminium alloy. Recent examples are the 500 Grand Prix Morbidelli and Kork Ballington's KR500 Kawasaki, although the latter is in fact a very complex structure some way removed from the idyllic simplicity of the word 'monocoque'.

The Morbidelli monocoque is an all-welded structure and the Kawasaki, particularly the 1981 version, had the petrol tank as a central structure connected to the engine and rear suspension by aluminium plates to which it was bolted and bonded. The four vertical plates, two outer and two inner, were bolted rigidly to the engine's gearbox castings, thereby acquiring the rigidity of the engine. The swinging arm pivot spindle ran through the plates and the rocker for the rear suspension pivoted between the two inner plates. The plates also provided support for the seat. Because the engine was so rigidly bolted to the frame an early version of the KR500 which suffered engine vibration problems was actually fitted with rubber mounted handlebars in an attempt to isolate the rider.

For 1982 Kawasaki redesigned their monocoque, making two very significant changes. Instead of a petrol tank monocoque made from sheet aluminium, a smaller spine was built from thicker plate. Although some petrol was contained within the spine, the required

In 1982 Kawasaki abandoned their true monocoque in favour of a box section, spine frame with separate fuel tank. The design of the 500 included a removable steering head block giving adjustable geometry.

fuel capacity necessitated a non-structural petrol tank to be built over the top. In the past the front of the petrol tank monocoque had always included the steering head but the 1982 design stopped short of the front forks and the steering head was held in an aluminium casting bolted to the front of the spine. This removeable steering head allowed the team to alter the rake of the forks by changing cast magnesium spacer plates, positioned between the steering head casting and the spine.

A modified version of the multi-plate, rear sub-frame system was retained and on this machine the outer plates were machined from a 1½″ (38mm) aluminium alloy block. This was needed to provide strengthening ribs and a milling or jig boring machine is the most

accurate way of ensuring a perfect relationship between the engine mounting holes and the suspension pivot points.

The 1980, '81 and '82 KR500 Kawasakis were relatively unsuccessful, but according to Kork Ballington this was mainly due to lack of engine power in the case of the 1982 machine. In 1981 the wheelbase had been too long and that seriously limited the motor cycle's manoeuvrability.

Although not monocoques, Yamaha have been building aluminium frames for their 500cc Grand Prix machines since 1980. For reasons the company has never explained, Yamaha have always used rectangular rather than round section tubing. There are several possible explanations: it has been suggested that because they made rectangular section swinging arms such

Although not a racing machine, the frame of Bimota's KB2 is a very fine and interesting design. It is completely different from the loop of tubing that normally surrounds the engine. In this case rigid, triangular structures pass either side. Likewise the steering head is surrounded by triangulated framework. This avoids the conflict of whether to splay the head tubes to cope with cornering forces or to maintain a narrow angle for braking stresses. The KB2 has both.

material was more freely available, but this seems an over simplification. It is more likely that Yamaha considers that the rectangular section is easier to join to other tubes and having unequal size the rectangular section tubing can be orientated to give the maximum strength in the desired direction. While round tubing offers greater resistance to tortional, or twisting, forces, square or rectangular tubing stands up better under bending. It would therefore suggest that Yamaha support the idea that braking forces, which tend to apply bending loads on the frame, are now greater than cornering forces, which apply more twisting action.

In 1981 Suzuki followed Yamaha's lead into rectangular section, aluminium frames, something that they too had been developing

for some time. In '82 Yamaha took development a step further with their V four engine, the OW61. Although it looked like a rather odd, twin loop or cradle frame, it was really more of a double spine. Because Yamaha feared that the double crankshaft, V arrangement would create serious vibration problems, the engine was well isolated from the frame by substantial rubber mountings. This meant that the engine could offer little as a stressed member and much greater reliance was placed on the frame's own rigidity.

Engines are quite often rubber mounted, but the particularly flexible nature of the new Yamaha system made the OW61 something rather special. The main structural members of the frame were two huge, rectangular tubes running from the steering head around the petrol tank to the swing arm. There was no obvious triangulation as such and, like the spine frame, the OW61 relied largely on the section of these tubes for its strength. Some support was derived from the lower frame rails, running down from the steering head and around the side of the engine. Cross bracing between these and the upper frame tubes was achieved by using a large cross member, made from two aluminium pressings welded together.

The back of the engine, which in most machines is used to maintain the rigidity around the swing arm, could obviously not be relied on. Large, rectangular section cross pieces were welded across the back of the frame. If further proof were needed that the engine was free to move within the frame, the designers found it necessary to build in a tie-rod from just below the swinging arm pivot to the lower, forward engine mounting point. This was vital to keep the engine from being pulled back in the frame by the tension in the drive chain under acceleration. Such movement would cause excessive chain wear. The tie-rod prevented this while still allowing the engine to shake up and down in its natural direction.

500cc and larger engines obviously place the greatest strain on their frames. They travel at the highest speeds, weigh the most and have the widest tyres, producing the greatest braking and cornering forces. In most cases the 250cc and 350cc, and to a great extent the 125cc, classes place similar if slightly lesser demands on their frames. Development budgets are always less in these classes and the private teams tend to settle for the easily available and reliable technology of the tubular steel frames. On the other hand, frame builders like the Chevalliers, Nico Bakker, Harris Performance Products and Bimota often produce fine examples of engineering.

Companies that produce frames for sale to the privateer have to consider that the individual's requirements differ from the factory teams and are not necessarily the same for the Club and National class rider as they are for the Grand Prix contender. Most small companies, if they have a successful reputation, will find themselves building frames to suit different needs as Steve Harris, of Harris Performance Products, explains:

"We have built frames for Barry Sheene and Jon Ekerold and these riders are looking for something that would be of little use to the privateer. The Grand Prix guys want a bike that is ultra-light. They want to win and it wouldn't really matter if the frame fell apart a couple of yards after crossing the finish line. But that's no good to the Club rider who wants a frame he can use for several years, and preferably one that he can crash without it being bent beyond repair."

Small companies and privateers are the mainstay of the 50cc and 80cc classes. Because the engines do not produce very much power and lightness is at a premium, the frames of the smallest machines are often rather different. The very successful Kreidlers

Constructing frames in rectangular section, aluminium tubing became popular from the start of the 1980s. It allows the use of lightweight tubing while maintaining a reasonable wall thickness. This example is the 1981 OW54 500cc Yamaha as raced by Barry Sheene and Kenny Roberts.

Fig. 1

Cofg = Centre of gravity
W = Weight of rider & machine
Bf =Breaking force or deceleration
R =Resultant of W and Bf

Fig. 2

This diagram shows the effect that raising or lowering the centre of gravity has on weight transfer. The same is true of acceleration.

developed a four main tube, spine frame with girder bridge-style cross bracing between the frame tubes. This takes full advantage of the fact that such engines are very small and it is possible to run frame tubes directly from the steering head to the swinging arm. Designers of the smallest capacity racing machines have the advantage that the engine size does not totally dictate its position in the frame. As Ron Williams suggested, engine position is absolutely crucial to the machine's performance. It affects everything.

Apart from the rider, the engine is by far the heaviest part of the motor cycle so its position has a lot of bearing on the centre of gravity. Moving the centre of gravity forward, putting more weight on the front wheel, will tend to make the motor cycle steer more heavily.

Not only is the centre of gravity's position fore and aft very important, so is its height above the ground. As explained in chapter 2, the higher the centre of gravity, the greater the effort required to change direction. The height of the centre of gravity also greatly affects the machine's performance under braking and acceleration (fig.1). It is quite obvious that the engine must be placed as close to the ground as possible. Unfortunately, the width of the engine, especially the large capacity units, causes problems when cornering. The wider the engine, the higher it must be raised in the frame. As the trend is always towards more and more tyre grip, providing better and better braking and more and more extreme cornering angles, the width of the engine and its effect on the centre of gravity assumes ever greater significance.

When the engine designer has done his best to make a powerful yet narrow unit, the frame specialist is then left to make the steering and suspension work with what he has been given. The problem is that the factors involved tend to militate against each other. The weight of the machine pitches it forward under braking, compressing the front suspension and altering the steering geometry. The front suspension must still be able to operate, keeping the front tyre in contact with the road as it rides over bumps and ripples, and the steering geometry must be so designed that it works not only with the suspension compressed but also when the suspension is fully extended as the weight is thrown back under acceleration.

Almost all racing machines use telescopic front forks (fig.3). These have been developed to a point where their theoretical limitations, i.e. lack of rigidity and heaviness, have been all but overcome. One unavoidable fact is that compressing the fork reduces the steering head angle and with it the trail. Both Bimota and Yamaha have tried passing the fork stanchions through the

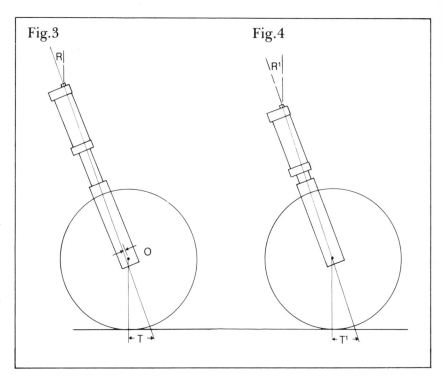

Fig.3   Fig.4

By making the fork tubes pass through the yokes at an angle the trail can be designed to remain constant as the forks are compressed.

yokes at an angle to the steering head so that compressing the forks has a smaller effect on the trail (fig.4). There is a limit to how big this angle can be because the greater the angle, the greater the tendency for the forks to be compressed under braking and the exercise becomes self-defeating. A more realistic answer is to provide some form of anti-dive mechanism that resists the tendency of the machine to nose-dive under braking.

Anti-dive mechanisms can be separated into two basic groups: they are either hydraulic or mechanical. The hydraulic systems restrict the oil damping passages and this slows the rate of compression of the front forks. The problem is that upsetting the damping hinders the smooth operation of the suspension. The early Suzuki hydraulic anti-dive virtually locked the suspension as the brakes were applied. This meant that the tyre might well be knocked off the road as the machine crested a bump. Suzuki soon modified the design to include a spring loaded valve so that sudden jolts would knock the valve off its seat and allow damping oil to pass. The system was also adjustable to give varying degrees of damping restriction, and hence anti-dive.

Suzuki universally adopted the design on both of their works and production racers and several of their road bike models. The system does have another drawback though. The force required to close off the damping holes is provided by the hydraulic pressure in the front brake system. This is created at the handlebar lever by the rider so not only must he squeeze the brake pads onto the disc, but he must also force the damping restrictor piston into the fork leg.

Honda's damping restrictor anti-dive, which was developed on the NR and NS500, goes one step better in that it does not require the rider to exert the pressure. This is provided by the torque reaction on the caliper mountings. The calipers pivot at their top mounting point on the fork leg and as they grab the disc they are pulled forward against the back of the fork leg and the lower mounting slides into the fork to operate the anti-dive. Although it seems to work well, this design still has a theoretical disadvantage in that it restricts free suspension movement under heavy braking.

There are fully mechanical anti-dive systems that allow completely free suspension movement while perfectly resisting the tendency to nose-dive. Such designs have been used by the Kawasaki works team on the KR500 and by several privateers and small manufacturers. By building a brake caliper mounting plate that pivots on or near the front wheel spindle the caliper will tend to turn in the direction of the rotation of the wheel as the brakes are applied. If the caliper mounting plate is then connected to the bottom fork yoke by a push rod, this tendency to rotate is turned into an anti-dive force. The amount of anti-dive, or rotational force, is directly proportional to the braking effect applied to the front wheel and as it is this that creates the weight transference and suspension compression, the two can be perfectly balanced.

By altering the leverage ratio, and hence the mechanical advantage that the brake plate exerts over the fork yoke, the degree of anti-dive can be adjusted. Depending upon the circuit and the rider's preference, the leverage may be adjusted to give 100% anti-dive and no suspension compression or, more usually, about 50% anti-dive so that the rider can easily feel the effect of the braking. Some degree of front suspension compression is actually an advantage as it lowers the centre of gravity, slightly decreasing the amount of weight transference and this helps to keep the rear tyre on the road under heavy braking.

Anti-dive devices have become so important because of the tremendous increase in braking performance. This is partly due to the fact that wide, 16″ wheels allow the tyre designers to put more rubber on the road and to make use of this more and more efficient brakes have been developed. One tendency is to use larger and larger diameter discs but there quickly comes a point, especially with 16″ wheels, where the brake caliper is almost rubbing on the wheel rim. At that point the designers look to creating more brake

Despite supposedly having an anti-dive system, the front forks of Randy Mamola's works Suzuki are totally compressed as he brakes for the corner.

swept area[10] by widening the disc surface so that bigger pads can be used. This has two problems: one, it requires greater lever pressure and two, the disc becomes considerably heavier. The alternative is to increase the pressure applied to the brake pad by the caliper. Unfortunately, this pressure must be supplied by the rider and there is obviously a limit to the force in his right hand.

The front brake lever moves a piston which forces fluid along the brake lines, thus transferring the force to the pistons in the brake calipers. The relative area of the piston in the handlebar master cylinder and the area of the pistons in the disc calipers dictates the relationship between the force applied by the rider and that exerted on the disc. By increasing the area of the caliper pistons, the force applied to the disc is in turn increased, but also increased is the distance that must be moved by the handlebar lever. As the pads wear during a race, this can give the brakes a very spongy feeling as pad wear is not always perfectly taken up by the extra hydraulic fluid drawn into the system from the master cylinder reservoir. One way of overcoming this limit on caliper piston size is to increase the number of pistons. Most racing machines' calipers have two pistons, one on each side of the disc. By doubling the number of pistons to four the piston area is increased without a corresponding increase in the distance that has to be travelled by the handlebar lever. It has also been found that there is an advantage to be gained in using pistons of unequal diameter.

Compared with the ineffective Suzuki damping restriction anti-dive, Kawasaki's mechanical system is much more efficient when it comes to maintaining suspension travel as can be seen here with Kork Ballington braking for the same corner as Randy Mamola in the other photograph.

Consider the disc passing through the caliper. If the second pair of pistons that it encounters are of a larger diameter than the first, they will force their end of the brake pad onto the disc harder than the smaller pistons. This creates a sort of wedge, but the passage of the disc between the two pads drives the wedge into the caliper, forcing the brake on harder. This wedge effect is almost like a servo[11] and gives more braking force for no greater effort.

At one time there was a fad for mounting the calipers in front of the fork legs so that they were cooled by the air but in fact it is the disc that gets hottest and is in most need of cooling. The calipers are therefore better positioned behind the fork legs, leaving more of the disc exposed. Temperature is very important to brake efficiency as brake pad material can only operate over a certain temperature range. If a high temperature range material is to be used, it may work very poorly when the brakes are cold and the converse is true. To keep the temperature within bounds, cool air must pass over the disc but with the wider and wider front tyres

10 The width of the disc braking surface, multiplied by its circumference. The larger the area, the more effective the brake.
11 Servo is a system whereby human action is aided by mechanical means. Normally, servo assisted brakes on cars etc. use air pressure.

being used, discs are increasingly being masked from the air flow. Several designers have experimented with ducts which force fresh air onto the discs.

The beautiful carbon fibre 250 Armstrong ready for the 1985 South African Grand Prix.

The discs themselves are also affected by temperature and they can be made from four materials: steel, cast iron, aluminium or carbon fibre.†. Aluminium has the advantage of light weight but the plasma spraying[12] that is necessary to provide a durable surface for the brake pads to bear on has proved incapable of withstanding the severe braking stresses exerted in 500cc and 1000cc machines although they are very popular in the smaller classes.

Cast iron discs are stable, reliable and provide an excellent braking surface but steel discs can be made thinner and therefore lighter. A problem with steel discs, however, is that they tend to warp if bolted rigidly to aluminium disc carriers. The differential expansion is overcome by providing the discs with a floating mounting on the carriers. Some teams mill slots across their discs to provide a cutting edge to clean the pad as the disc passes. This can create high pad wear but it does prevent glazing[13] by taking a light skim off the surface. To the same end discs are often drilled and this obviously helps to make then lighter as well. It should be noted that the holes must not be chamfered as it is their sharp, cutting edges that do the work.

Cast iron is often used to make ventilated discs which can cool themselves quickly, thanks to the extra surface area and the air that is forced through the radial ventilations by the spinning of the disc. Suzuki have long used a ventilated disc on the rear of their RG500 because it is a compact unit that might overheat as it is shrouded by the fairing and the rider's legs.

Raymond Roche on the Marlboro Yamaha at the Spanish Grand Prix.

Carbon fibre or rather carbon carbon discs as they are often called because they contain no resin are even lighter than plasma sprayed aluminium. They are still under development and durability has been a problem. Carbon carbon pads are used with carbon discs and Lockheed developed a peripheral disc that bolts to the rim instead of the centre of the wheel giving it more mechanical advantage.

Although the rear brake does very little work compared with the front brake, it can be quite important, depending on the rider's style. Under heavy, straight line braking the rear wheel will be barely touching the ground and very little brake pressure would lock it. The rider is much more likely to use the back brake to steady

12 Applied molten material to an object by firing particles of that material through a high temperature gas flame. The molten particles adhere to the surface of the object, forming a coating.
13 A polishing of the pad to a smooth, glossy finish which occurs when the pad is used at the wrong operating temperature.
† Carbon fibre – see chapter 12.

the machine if he feels it is hopping about on the road at the approach to a corner. In wet weather he is much more inclined to dab the back brake in an emergency while cornering than grab the front. A rear end slide might be tricky to control, but losing the front end in the wet would virtually guarantee disaster.

There are three ways of mounting the back brake caliper and each has a significant effect on what happens when that brake is applied. If the mounting plate is anchored directly to the swinging arm and the brake is applied while the wheel is passing over bumps, then the tyre feels a relative acceleration and deceleration with respect to the tarmac as it rises and falls. This can cause the tyre to skid and tends to make the rear wheel hop and judder. To avoid this the brake plate can be anchored to the frame by a tie rod and be allowed to pivot around the rear wheel spindle. If the tie-rod starts off above the swinging arm and is bolted to the frame, also above the swinging arm, or, equally, both positions are below the swinging arm, then braking will have the effect of extending the suspension. This has the advantage of forcing the rear tyre onto the ground which provides better grip for braking but it also pushes the rear of the motor cyle upwards, raising the centre of gravity and adding to the weight transference onto the front suspension. If on the other hand the tie-rod crosses the swing arm, the opposite happens. The rear of the machine is pulled down and the tyre, up. Either method alleviates the hop and judder of the rigid mounting and must be left to personal preference. Marco Lucchinelli has always preferred the cross-over, floating mounting while most riders, including Barry Sheene and Randy Mamola, prefer the parallelogram.

Rear braking performance and rear suspension are much less closely connected than front braking and suspension. Rear suspension is most important after the back brake has been let off and the machine is cornering and/or accelerating. Ron Williams pays a great deal of attention to rear suspension: "The racing motor cycle spends most of its time with the power on. Apart from heavy braking which occurs mostly in a straight line, the racing motor cycle spends most of its time with the weight on the rear wheel under acceleration. It doesn't matter if the front end shakes its head a little bit as long as the rider is able to apply the power to the road."

The job of suspension is to keep the tyres in contact with the tarmac. When the wheel hits a bump it will naturally be thrown into the air but for the opposing action of the suspension springs. A very large problem with today's racing motor cycle is that the effective weight of the wheel, tyre and brake is very high. This is

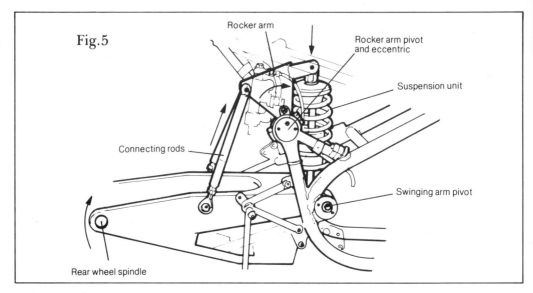

Fig.5

Rocker arm

Rocker arm pivot
and eccentric

Suspension unit

Connecting rods

Swinging arm pivot

Rear wheel spindle

Rocker arm rear suspension like this Chevallier design can be designed to give a rising suspension rate.

true of both the front and the rear wheels. As designers use lighter and lighter metals, aluminium, titanium and magnesium, to reduce the weight of the engine and frame etc., the wheel systems, with their brakes and tyres getting larger and larger, take up a greater and greater proportion of the total weight. This has the unfortunate effect that when one of the wheels passes over a bump, it has a greater tendency to push the motor cycle up in the air than the motor cycle has the ability to push it back on the ground. This makes the relationship between sprung and unsprung[14] weight important.

With a machine such as Honda's NS500 which has a very low all-up weight, the engineers went to considerable lengths to build the lightest possible wheel. The rims were aluminium, as were the spokes; the hubs were cast in magnesium and the wheels were bolted together with titanium bolts. They even tried carbon fibre spokes and rims in an attempt to reduce the weight still further. Most machines use cast magnesium alloy wheels and carbon fibre discs must surely be considered for their weight saving properties as they have already been used in the aircraft field.

Whatever the weight of the wheels etc., the rear suspension still has a considerable job to do. A road racing machine cannot have twelve inches of suspension travel like a motocrosser because the changes that they would bring to the position of the centre of gravity and the steering geometry would be impossible to live with.

14 The weight of the machine and rider can be split into the sprung and the unsprung. Sprung weight includes the engine, frame and rider etc. and this is separated from the unsprung weight of tyres, wheels and brakes by the suspension springs. There is a slight complication concerning parts of the suspension like the swing arm, which is connected to both the frame and the wheel. It must be largely considered as unsprung weight as its motion must be controlled by the springs.

Suspension travel must be limited to a maximum of about 6" (152mm) and would ideally be less if the springing and damping system could control the wheel. The suspension must allow the wheel to move relatively freely over the first half of its movement, then meet with progressively stiffer resistance which builds up so that the wheel and suspension never come smashing into the limit of the suspension unit's travel. This progressively rising rate of suspension resistance is necessary so that the wheel can be allowed to be moved up and down freely at first to accommodate small irregularities in the road surface as the machine races along in a straight line. Yet the suspension must be able to resist the addition of the considerable centrifugal force created during cornering.

The rising spring rate might be accomplished by producing a coil spring whose windings vary in strength along its length. Such a spring is almost impossibly difficult to make, particularly to any degree of consistency. The best that could reasonably be done would be to use two or more springs of different grades. Practically speaking there would only be room for two springs and this is not subtle enough for the demands of racing. There is the added problem that, as the suspension unit moves from working on the lower spring rate to the higher, the damping rate would remain the same. Damping[15] must match the spring rate or the wheel cannot be properly controlled.

The answer is to link the suspension unit to the wheel movement in such a way that the mechanical advantage exerted by the unit on the wheel increases as the wheel rises. In this way a single rate spring is used but effectively a rising rate is achieved and the damping experiences the same change as the spring.

When virtually all motor cycles have twin suspension units mounted directly between the swing arm and the frame, a small degree of rising rate can be achieved by leaning the units forward. As the wheel rose, the angle between the swing arm and the axis of the suspension unit would go from less than 90° to 90° and hence the mechanical advantage would increase, although only slightly. Yamaha introduced a cantilever[16] suspension which gave more rear wheel movement for a given amount of suspension unit travel, but still only a very marginally rising rate. It was the rocker arm system used by Bimota and, to tremendous effect, by Kawasaki on

15 An undamped spring will, in theory at least, oscillate, or bounce, for ever. If a motor cycle's suspension was undamped hitting one bump would cause it to bounce again and again but damping acts as a drag on the spring's movement. This is normally accomplished by a small piston which runs up and down inside a bore, filled with hydraulic fluid. The piston squeezes the fluid through tiny holes. The drag is designed to be less on the spring's compression than it is on extension and this cuts down on multiple rebounds. Damping must be perfectly matched to the springing and both must suit the rider, machine and circuit (see chapter 7).
16 Cantilever is defined as an arm or beam fixed at one end and free at the other.

Alain Chevallier's frame design, pictured here, is as successful as any produced by Ron Williams but the two men disagree widely about certain areas of frame design. Chevallier has no triangle formed over the top of the engine and his frame tubes do not cross behind the steering head. He produces triangles with removable cross braces; Chevallier's engines are rubber mounted and play no part as stressed members. "The engine cases are not strong enough and I have seen far too many crankshaft failures when rigidly mounted engines are distorted in a twisting frame." Chevallier's thinking serves to prove that there are few absolute rules in frame design.

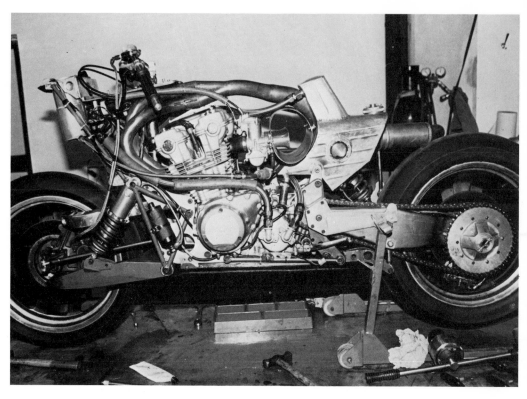

their multiple World Championship-winning KR250 and 350, that started the ball rolling as far as true rising rate suspensions were concerned. By altering the relationship between the swing arm, the connecting rods, two arms of the rocker, its pivot point and the suspension unit (fig.5) any desired rising rate curve can be created. In many systems it becomes impossible to see, just by looking at them, how the effective spring rate varies as the wheel moves. This is complicated by the fact that the relationship between the distance moved and effective spring rate is a square. If the rear wheel moves two units and the suspension unit compresses one unit, then the spring must be four times as strong as would be needed if the two moved in a one to one ratio.

The variations that have been explored in search of that perfect curve are numerous. Kawasaki developed a second generation system which they call, like the first, Uni-Trak. This was used on the KR500 and employed a triangulated swing arm and a short connecting rod to the rocker. Suzuki have preferred to call their system a Full Floater, this being a variation on Kawasaki's original theme but with the lower end of the suspension unit mounted on the swing arm. Honda chose to pivot their rocker arm in the swing arm and called this system 'Pro-Link'. It took Yamaha a long time to get away from their basic cantilever system because, like all the

The Honda-engined, Elf Experimental is a superb example of a radical departure from conventional frame steering design. The engine cases are almost solely responsible for supporting the front and rear suspension. The steering is car-style hub centre, supported between two single-sided swinging arms working as a parallelogram. This Endurance racing machine has worked well but it will be a long time before the majority of racing motor cycles follow its example.

Japanese manufacturers, they quickly adopted the idea used in racing for many of their production road and trail machines. Having done so it was unpolitic to admit that it could be improved upon by altering their works racer.

Yamaha experimented in 1981 with a small rocker, connected to the top of the cantilever swing arm. This proved unsuccessful and was dropped. The company completely revolutionised their cantilever system in 1982 when they unveiled the V four engined OW61. In this machine the suspension unit was mounted horizontally across the top of the gearbox and compressed at each end by a rocker arm. These arms pivoted about axes vertically into the frame. The rockers were L-shaped so that the connecting rods running from them to the swing arm pushed forward and then they turned in on the suspension unit.

Another method of creating a rising spring rate is the use of gas pressure. This can be used in both the front forks and rear suspension units. A captured volume of gas exerts a pressure which increases as its volume is decreased. This method is limited in the same way as the multi-rate spring because damping does not change with the air pressure. Gas pressure is used in many suspension units because the gas can absorb the change in volume within the unit as the unit is compressed. It can also be used to resist the damping fluid's tendency to aerate.[17] As the gas, whether it be air or nitrogen as are most commonly used, is repeatedly compressed and decompressed it heats up. With this heat the gas tries to expand and its pressure increases. If this heating is not prevented the suspension unit will virtually lock up solid. Remote reservoirs of extra gas limit this tendency, particularly when they are mounted in the cool air stream. Heat also has a debilitating effect on the damping fluid which becomes less viscous as the temperature rises and hence the damping efficiency is then reduced. Damper fluid will be heated by friction as it is repeatedly squeezed through the damping holes. This heat must be allowed to escape if the suspension unit damping is to remain consistent. Suspension units which are placed near to the engine or next to exhaust pipes cannot be expected to work reliably for long.

As engine power continues to increase, tyres provide more and more grip and the relationship between sprung and unsprung weight grows worse, the suspension designer must be more and more ingenious to enable the rider to keep the power applied to the road.

---

17 As damping fluid is forced through the control orifices, bubbles are generated which destroy its homogeneity and its effectiveness as a consistent damping medium.

6
Tyres

Riding a motor cycle at speed often feels very much like flying an aeroplane or, better, like being a bird. The rider and the machine are one unit, going slower or faster at will, turning left or right with the added dimension of leaning into the corner adding to the sensation of speed while keeping in perfect balance, making it all seem completely effortless.

Motor cycle racing certainly is a three dimensional experience yet in fact, in purely physical terms it takes place in two dimensions with the plane limitation of the tarmac beneath. The motor cycle swoops and curves, seemingly without restriction, the one thing

Kenny Roberts, deep in discussion with Dunlop's Peter Ingley.

tying it to the ground is the rubber of the tyres, making its tiny contact with the road. But it is not a limitation: it is essential as it provides all the other movement. When the rider demands it, the motor cycle will accelerate, brake, lean and turn but only as long as the rubber's fingernail grip with the grains of the tarmac is maintained.

What is a racing motor cycle tyre? Is it just black, rubbery and round? Certainly since the practical pneumatic tyre was invented by John Boyd Dunlop in 1888, the basic principle has remained the same. But even the casual observer must have noticed that racing tyres have lost their tread pattern and have increased in size. These simple observations show scant regard for the sophisticated chemical and structural engineering developments.

A 500cc engine might take half a mile (0.8 km) to accelerate the machine to its maximum speed of perhaps 180 mph (290 kph) and yet the front brakes will slow it to a crawl in a matter of 300 yards (0.27 km). Braking or accelerating the front or back tyre are hard at work and during cornering both are subjected to the tremendous centrifugal forces created by turning a motor cycle through a tight corner at speed. If the bike is leaning over at 45 degrees then the centrifugal force is equal to the weight of the machine (see chapter 2, page 39). Imagine trying to pick up a 500cc motor cycle complete with rider yourself and you can see the frictional force generated at the tyre contact patches.[1]

At any point racing tyre design is battling to keep up with engine development. At the Daytona 200 meeting in March 1982 Dunlop unveiled the KR106, at eight inches the widest motor cycle tyre available.

If it were just a case of making wider and wider tyres the designers' job would be simple but when the motor cycle leans over the contact patch moves round the tyre. As the contact patch moves towards the inside of the corner so the machine has to be leaned further to maintain the correct balance of forces (see chapter 2, page 39). Wide tyres are also heavy and of course this is unsprung weight and it is rotating so it affects gyroscopic reactions (chapter 2, page 42). In any case the simple law of friction, $F = \mu C$, involves no area term stating that the frictional force (F) can only be equal to the co-efficient of friction (μ) multiplied by the normal contact force (C) which is equal and opposite to the weight of the body. In most cases μ cannot exceed 1 so therefore the frictional force cannot be greater than the weight of the machine and rider. If this were true no machine could lean over more than 45 degrees. They

1   The patch of rubber in contact with the road at any one time. Its size varies with the speed of the tyre, the weight placed on the wheel and the lean of the machine.

do though, and this is because the rubbers used in modern racing tyres work beyond the simple law of friction, benefitting from an effective μ greater than 1 and from an area term in the equation that means that wider tyres give more grip.

The friction generated between the tyre and road can be split into three parts: the almost insignificant bonds between the molecules of rubber and the molecules of tarmac as they touch on a microscopic level and the much greater friction generated by the rubber actually moulding around the grains of tarmac, and being deformed as the tyre tries to slide across the road. The third part of the friction is the actual tearing of the rubber as the tarmac cuts through the molecules.

The rubber compound must be so formulated that it can mould itself around the grains of tarmac and it can do this because the chains of molecules are flexible to a degree. If the rubber is too soft it will deform too easily and the tyre will slide as the rubber just flows over the surface of the tarmac. To prevent this the rubber is made stiffer by cross linkages going from one chain of molecules to another. The cross linkages must not be too strong or the rubber will be too hard and unable to mould itself at all. Here the temperature of the tyre plays an important part because at higher temperatures the bonds between the molecules are made more flexible. Unfortunately, increased temperature also reduces the tensile strength[2] of the bonds and this means that the tarmac is more likely to cut through the rubber which results in rapidly increased wear.

The temperature generated in the tyre comes from two sources: the first is the deformation and restoration of the tread rubber as the tyre moves across the surface. This happens even as the tyre rolls but if it is forced to spin or slide the deformation occurs much more quickly and the hysteresis[3] generates more heat.

The second cause of heat generation is the flexing of the casing itself to which the tread rubber is bonded. It is the casing that gives the tyre its shape, its profile. The profile must be designed to put the maximum area of rubber on the road at the desired time and the casing must be capable of maintaining this profile as the loads impressed upon it vary in strength and direction. A well-designed casing will, in fact, deform just the right amount producing more contact patch area than there would be with a perfectly rigid casing.

Fig. 1

Casing construction for crossply, bias belted and radial tyres.

CROSS PLY

BIAS BELTED

RADIAL

2   Tensile strength is the resistance to braking when an object is pulled apart under pure tension.
3   The lagging of an effect behind the cause of the effect i.e. the rubber is deformed but then takes a period of time to bounce back and the hysteresis loop can be plotted graphically showing the degree of deformation with an applied force as the force is taken through a complete cycle of increasing and decreasing values. The area of the loop measures the energy dissipated through the cycle.

A rear tyre may suffer additional heat build-up if rearward facing exhaust pipes running under the seat create a mass of hot air which is trapped and passes its heat to the tyre.

A tyre casing is constructed in layers, or plies, which resemble a cloth woven with almost all warp and very little weft. The thread of the plies can be made of rayon, nylon, polyester or polymamide or a mixture. They offer a variety of strength to weight ratios and fatigue resistance.

The plies are laid across the tyre form at an angle to each other (see fig.1). This crossply design is absolutely vital to casing performance. It largely dictates the tyre's contribution to machine stability and the degree of flexion built into the casing. The smaller the angle between the plies and the nearer they lie to running along the circumference of the tyre the less flexion there is in the casing.

A compromise, which allows a stiffer tread area to be combined with a flexible side wall, is the bias belted tyre. This uses a crossply construction but with a belt of different material, usually laid around the circumference underneath the tread. The bias belt keeps the tread rubber in contact with the road while allowing the tyre wall to flex, giving the machine's suspension an easier time. Tyres that do not flex sufficiently in the side wall often result in pattering because the motor cycle's suspension, and particularly its damping, cannot cope with the high frequency ripples and bumps. Pattering can also be generated in a tyre because of the stick slip situation that occurs when the tyre is right on the limit of adhesion. Alain Chevallier, for example, has found that when setting up the suspension for his own team's machines, Dunlop tyres allow a greater latitude. "If we are using Michelin tyres, the rear suspension must be set perfectly if it is to work well. The Dunlop tyres seem to offer better suspension characteristics themselves and allow the suspension a greater range over which it is still effective."

The biggest single change to occur in racing tyre design in the 80s was the advent of the successful radial tyre. Previously it had been thought that radial construction was not suitable for motor cycle tyre construction because there was too much side wall flex to control the profile during cornering. Pirelli pioneered the concept of using the radial motorcycle tyre and the other major manufacturers followed suit as they developed designs that controlled the profile and flexibility in part by using shorter sidewalls. The advantage is that the radial flexibility can produce a larger contact patch for a given tyre size and profile without sacrificing stability and with a bonus weight saving. The larger contact patch means that a softer compound can be used for better grip without excessive wear.

At the edge of the tyre the plies wrap under and around the bead wire which is a loop running the complete circumference of each bead edge. The bead wire on a racing tyre is usually made from steel and this has two important functions. It provides the correct fit between the tyre bead and the motor cycle's wheel and it prevents the tyre from being split during fitting as it is levered over the wheel rim. The centrifugal force generated by the spinning tyre would tend to make it "grow" away from the rim and the bead wire must prevent this or the tyre would be able to move around on the rim. If the torque of the engine, or the machine's brakes, were able to turn the tyre on the wheel rim it might deflate with disastrous results.

The threat of tyres moving on rims has quite often been countered by the use of rim screws. Small self-tapping screws are inserted into the tyre bead rubber through holes in the wheel rim. Rim screws should not be necessary if the bead is correctly designed and accurately made but it is a problem of fine balance as, if the bead is too small a diameter it will be virtually impossible to fit the tyre onto the rim. It stands to reason that the wheel must be equally accurately made if the correct fit is to be maintained. The use of a lubricant which eases tyre fitting can upset the balance as it might reduce the friction between the bead and the wheel. Even Dunlop, who used to use bead lubricant when fitting tyres, had an embarrassing experience at Imola in 1981 when Randy Mamola's rear tyre suffered a slight loss of balance due to the tyre turning on the wheel. Since then they have used pure water and the problem has not recurred.

Tyre profiles, or the cross sectional view of the tyre, have changed greatly in recent years. One of the ways of describing a tyre's profile is through its aspect ratio which relates to the percentage difference between the height and width of a tyre's section. For example, if a tyre section height is 3.5 in. (89mm) and this is measured from the base of the bead to the highest point of the tread, and its width is 4.3 in. (109mm) then the aspect ratio is $\frac{3.5}{4.3}$ = 0.814 or 81%. Tyres nave got wider and flatter over the last two decades with their aspect ratios changing from approximately 85% to 50%. Here, the two major competitors differ greatly. Dunlop's KR106 rear tyre has an aspect ratio of 50%, while Michelin's comparable tyre has a 72% ratio. Dunlop use the larger aspect ratio tyres to provide a greater contact patch area while Michelin rely on more flexible casing constructions which allow their tyres to flatten out more on the road.

Aspect ratio is not the whole profile story because profiles may be virtually triangular, like the KR106, or more rounded as favoured by Michelin. The idea behind the triangular nature of the KR106 is best explained by Dunlop's Grand Prix tyre designer, Peter Ingley:

"There were two major criteria to be considered when designing the 106: improved change of direction and steering and greater contact patch exiting a corner. The greater contact patch gives us more licence to run softer compounds or gives existing compounds greater life".

In comparison the Michelin's rounder profile gives a smoother transition from upright to full lean.

The tyre's profile is not only dictated by its moulded shape, but also by the width of the wheel rim to which it is fitted. Quite simply the wider the wheel rim, the flatter the profile but the tyre is designed to fit a limited range of rims and in going outside the design recommendations is bound to have ill effects. For example, if one of Dunlop's common KR108 rear slicks is used on a 250cc or 350cc machine, then a 2.5 in. or 3.00 in. rear rim is recommended and that suits their 375/500–18 tyre. If such a tyre is used on too wide a wheel rim, say 3.5 in., the profile is so flattened that, at extreme angles of lean, the rider will be running off the edge of the tyre. Too wide a rim can, in some cases, make the rear tyre steer the machine, as at high speed it will have a tendency to go straight on. If too narrow a rim is used then the tyre's profile will be well rounded and cornering may not use all the tread available. This means that not all the contact patch is being used.

If the ultimate aim was to achieve larger and larger contact patches then machines of every capacity would be fitted with huge tyres but the desire to keep the contact patch as near as possible to the centre line of the machine when cornering and to minimise weight keeps tyre width down. It is always important to match the tyre to the performance of the machine. While the large, more powerful machines have wide tyres, smaller, lighter motor cycles benefit from lighter, narrower tyres. Apart from anything else friction is generated merely by the rolling of the tyre and this drag on wheel rotation is something that the small capacity machines can well do without.

The front wheel in particular is affected detrimentally if too large a tyre is used. It makes the machine very heavy to steer into corners because of the high rotating mass, the movement of the contact patch and the self-centring effect of the tyre. The search for a wider front tyre to provide a greater area for braking has led to the introduction of 16 in. wheels to replace the normal 18 in. to try to reduce the rotating mass. The pros and cons of such front tyres are not clear cut. The very fact of reducing the rolling radius of the tyre alters the steering geometry of the machine and if a motor cycle, designed to run on 18 in. wheels with a given steering rake and trail (see chapter 2, page 51), is fitted with a smaller wheel both the rake and trail will automatically be reduced. This will certainly make the motor cycle steer more quickly and lightly but the same result could be achieved by designing the steering geometry correctly in the first place. Assuming that the steering geometry has been designed with a particular size wheel in mind, the 16 in. tyre may still offer some advantages as Graeme Crosby has pointed out: "A 16 inch tyre makes you feel as if you can dive very deep into the corner with the brakes on and scrub off a lot of speed. I think it takes more horsepower to drive round a corner, though". Kenny Roberts, on the other hand, definitely prefers the larger wheel: "I like an 18 inch front tyre and the stability it gives. The problem is to get the right profile which will make the steering quick and light, yet allow you to use the large contact patch."

Peter Ingley, for one, is not convinced that there are many fundamental advantages in 16 in. wheels. "The only thing a 16 inch wheel does for you is make the machine steer faster. They have less dynamic mass and they alter the steering geometry. On certain motor cycles, braking is improved but it is only better because it alters the ratio between the wheel and brake diameter. An 18 inch tyre is more stable and gives a more confident feel. If you put them on line, there they tend to stay without wandering".

Indeed, having a smaller diameter tyre must, of course, slightly reduce the contact patch as it reduces circumference. To get the advantage of less rotating mass yet retain the steering stability of the eighteen inch tyre Dunlop developed seventeen inch front tyres which Kenny Roberts used on several occasions in '83 and Eddie Lawson employed to win the World Championship in '84. Michelin have also used seventeen inch rims particularly at the back with their low profile radial tyres so that the rolling diameter is very similar to a high profile sixteen. This saves a good deal of weight in the rubber of the sidewall.

Tyre compounds that mould themselves around the grains of tarmac work best on a clean, dry road. Anything that comes between the rubber and the tarmac greatly reduces the grip: dust, oil or shredded rubber lying on the surface is a tremendous hindrance to the tyre technicians and the riders. These things must be tolerated, but water presents a far greater problem and is countered by treaded tyres in an attempt to cut through the film of water which separates rubber from road.

Slick, untreaded tyres provide the greatest contact patch area for dry weather use but would ride up on any layer of water, causing

Dunlop's full wet tyre, KR144. The rain grooves must be large enough to carry away large quantities of water yet the block pattern that remains must be rigid enough so that the tyre is stable and does not wander off line.

complete separation from the tarmac and aquaplaning. By reducing the surface area with a tread pattern, the tyre designer effectively increases the pressure on the raised sections of tyre, pushing them through the water and onto the road.

Designing an effective tread pattern is very difficult indeed. The water channels must be sufficiently large to clear a fair volume of water from underneath the tyre and prevent an accumulation which would create a wedge and lift the tyre off the road. But if the grooves are too large, there is too little tread pattern and not enough rubber touches the road to provide sufficient friction. The shape of the tread pattern is important so that the blocks of rubber will distort just enough to provide a cutting edge to clear the water without being so unstable that they squirm and 'walk', causing the tyre to wander from its intended course.

Wet weather tyre compounds are generally softer than dry weather slicks. The tyres are cooled by the water and must be soft so that they can still mould around the tarmac where contact exists. Because of the soft compound and the blocks of tread that distort, a wet weather tyre will quickly overheat as the track surface begins to dry. Intermediate tyres offer a compromise between the two extremes. With a harder compound that can more readily cope with the cornering speeds and the power applied during dry weather racing, they still have small rain grooves to dissipate a certain amount of surface moisture. In the situation where the tarmac is damp, but there is no water lying on the surface, it is almost always best to use a slick tyre as it can still reach its working temperature and there is no chance of aquaplaning. Circuits tend to dry on the racing line but the threat of further rain will normally cause riders to choose an intermediate pattern and compound.

Intermediate and wet weather tyres normally have moulded patterns but during development, or in particular circumstances peculiar to a race track, or with a new machine, treaded tyres may be hand cut from suitable slicks. This is done by stencilling the rain groove pattern on the tyre and then a hot wire gun is used to cut the grooves (see page 155). Such an operation is obviously labour intensive. A full rain tyre will take 5 hours to cut. When slick tyres were first introduced in 1972 grooves were sometimes cut even in dry weather to make the tread move around more if there was difficulty in warming up properly. Improvements in casing construction and compound chemistry have now made this unnecessary. The only marks to be found on modern slicks are the holes in the tread which give an indication of the tyre wear.

Along with slick tyres a recent step in tyre development has been the wide use of tubeless tyres. The inner tube, the sole purpose of

Freddie Spencer explores the possibilities provided by the radial Michelin tyres fitted to his 250 Honda.

which is to contain the air which pressurizes the tyre, adds to the weight of the tyre and friction is generated as the tyre distorts and the two rub together. As long as the tyre bead provides a good seal with the wheel rim (and the wheel itself must be airtight) then there is no reason why the tyre cannot be run without a tube. Apart from the reduction in weight and heat, there is an added safety factor: if a tubeless tyre turns on the rim, there may be a gradual loss of air pressure but a tubed tyre that rotates will drag the tube with it, pulling the valve out of the tube with a sudden, total loss of pressure.

Experimental wet weather tyres are cut by hand. It is a skilled, time consuming operation using a hot wire cutting tool to follow a stencilled pattern.

Tubeless tyres are likely to deflate at a slower rate when punctured. If pierced by a sharp object the rubber tends to turn in on itself, sealing the hole. An inner tube is not thick enough to do this. Tubeless tyres, though, can cause the fitter to scream with anguish because the bead does not seal properly until the tyre is partially inflated. Very often the air will escape as fast as it is pumped in.

Before it can be used, the tyre must be inflated to the correct pressure. This depends on the size of the tyre, type of casing and the weight of the machine. Too low a pressure and the tyre will over deform and overheat. Too high a pressure and the tyre will not deform enough to give the right contact patch.

After the tyre has been fitted and inflated it must be balanced. No tyre, and very few wheels, have their weight perfectly evenly distributed around the circumference. When the wheel is spun at high speed, the centrifugal force acting on a heavy spot causes vibration which can acutally lift the wheel off the road once every revolution. At the very least it makes life difficult for the suspension and gives uneven tyre wear. A heavy spot on the wheel or tyre is counteracted by sticking a suitable weight to the opposite side of the rim. The tyre is balanced by the fitter who places the wheel on a spindle and this is placed in freely rotating bearings. Any heavy spot will turn the wheel until it lies at the bottom. The fitter then sticks lead weight to the top of the wheel rim until the imbalance is removed.

Out of balance front wheels are very obvious to the rider because the vibration can be felt through the handlebars. Rear tyre imbalance is disguised by the chain running around the sprockets and for this reason some people do not bother to balance rear wheels.

At circuits where tyres over heating may be a problem due to very high speeds and hard acceleration and braking, such as Imatra in Finland and the Portrush North West 200 circuit in Northern Ireland, pure nitrogen may be used instead of air.

Nitrogen is an inert gas which reacts better in such circumstances, giving virtually no increase in pressure. As increased pressure generates heat, this is obviously a disadvantage.

The tyre technician will keep a close eye on tyre temperature during practice. He does this with an electrical thermometer which has a sharp metal probe which can be inserted into the tread rubber. The reading is given on a dial; a typical maximum reading for a modern racing slick is 248°F (120°C). Above this point tyre wear will be rapid. A minimum temperature will be around 176°F (80°C) below which changing to a softer compound would be recommended. Although air temperature has little effect on the temperature of the tyre, the tarmac temperature will make a difference and the tyre technician will sometimes use his temperature probe on the track surface if he wishes to make certain as to how that is affecting his tyre temperature as opposed to the working of the compound and the casing.

When racing takes place in cold conditions with very low track temperatures, it may be difficult to raise the slick to an operating temperature without using such a soft compound that would cause

A selection of Michelin racing tyres: full wets on the left, intermediate tyres on the right and slicks behind.

rapid tyre wear. Warm up laps are always allowed immediately before the start of each race so that the tyre has a chance to reach a reasonable temperature before the important first racing lap. Unfortunately, if the riders then have to stand on the grid in cold weather the tyres may quickly cool. Being black, they radiate heat quickly in such conditions. Quite often organisers are slack in this respect. When track temperatures are cold, a tyre may only heat up in the middle and one side. If on a clockwise track which has perhaps only one left hand corner, that left hander can be very dangerous indeed because rubber is a poor conductor of heat and the rider trying to negotiate this corner at the same speed as the right handers can come to grief. This is especially so as the left side of the tyre can cool down from one lap to the next.

A brand new tyre must not only be warmed up but also 'scrubbed in'. A certain amount of lubricant is sometimes used in moulding the tyres and this must be cleared from the surface before good grip is provided. More than this, scrubbing in cuts away the outer smooth skin of the rubber which is slightly harder than the rest and allows the molecular chains to start working. Tyre experts try to dissuade riders from scrubbing in tyres with a file or glass paper or from spinning the rear wheel while holding the machine stationary on the front brake. This sets up the wrong wear pattern in the rubber and can detract from the effectiveness of the compound.

The wear patterns that can be seen on any slick tell the tyre technician a good deal about the way it is working. Typically, the middle of the tread will have lines running across it, showing the way that the rubber has been scuffed off under heavy braking and these lines turn to run along the circumference of the tread as braking effect decreases and cornering forces increase towards the edge of the tyre and maximum lean. Large ridges on the tyre indicate too high a wear rate, less than maximum friction and a harder compound is required. Sometimes tyres appear completely smooth; this may be because the compound is not reaching its working temperature but certain track surfaces can be very deceptive. The Brno Grand Prix circuit in Czechoslovakia and the Scarborough Park circuit are typical public road tracks where accumulations of oil and diesel fuel impregnate the surface, making it very slippery and preventing the usual wear patterns from being set up.

Donington Park, on the other hand, is a circuit with a surface that is very abrasive. It cuts through tyres, giving a high wear rate without providing higher than average grip.

Tyre construction and compounding is certainly advanced but competition forces the tyre companies to push the compromises of tyre life and grip to the limit. Even though a tyre may still have adequate tread depth left on it, its best performance can still have passed. Kork Ballington describes the process of tyre wear during a Grand Prix: "Even though there is a warm up lap before the race you must still take it easy for several laps to allow the tyre to warm up completely. After about four laps a new tyre will be working really well and that will last for about another four laps when the tyre is still working at its very best. Then it might be as early as lap eight you begin to notice a slight deterioration in the performance." The 500 class is particularly hard on tyres, especially at the rear because of the power produced. It is by no means unusual to see the leading riders pacing themselves below maximum lap times so that the tyres do not go off leaving themselves a few laps flat out performance to decide the race in the closing stages.

A tyre that has been raised to full working temperature during the course of a race may never give maximum performance again even though enough tread remains. The life of the tyre depends on many things but works riders will never use the same tyre for two Grands Prix. The privateer who has to buy his own tyres may be forced financially to accept second best and Stu Avant is well aware of the problems: "I normally use the race tyre from one Grand Prix in practice for the next or if that is too worn out I try and buy a second hand tyre from someone. It makes it hard because you are trying to qualify in a good position against works riders who seem to get a new tyre for every practice session. I then buy a new tyre and scrub it in for the race. On most circuits the new tyre makes up about a second a lap."

For all the work the tyre companies put in in their laboratories to produce theoretically better tyres, it is down to the rider to take them out on the circuit and find out if they allow him to go faster. After racing virtually all his working life with Goodyear, Kenny Roberts changed to Dunlop at the beginning of 1982. He took the square four Yamaha to Laguna Seca to do some initial testing: "We chose to go to Laguna because I know every inch of the track. I know how the bike and the tyres should perform. This year particularly I wanted to improve the speed at which I could change direction, flicking from right to left and from vertical to maximum lean. Laguna is good for that because there are a lot of corners where you brake and pitch it in hard. It also has corners like the Corkscrew where you have to go really quick from left to right. At Laguna I was just interested in the feeling and wasn't looking for traction. You can sort that out later with the compounds and it varies from track to track. But I wanted to get the profile right."

7

Circuits

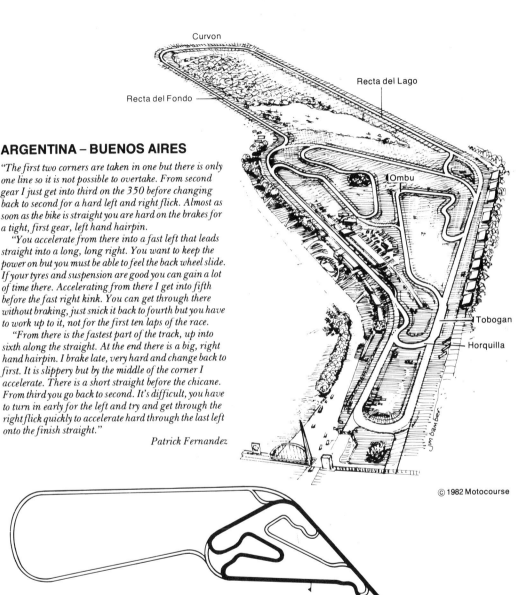

Curvon

Recta del Lago

Recta del Fondo

ARGENTINA – BUENOS AIRES

"The first two corners are taken in one but there is only one line so it is not possible to overtake. From second gear I just get into third on the 350 before changing back to second for a hard left and right flick. Almost as soon as the bike is straight you are hard on the brakes for a tight, first gear, left hand hairpin.

"You accelerate from there into a fast left that leads straight into a long, long right. You want to keep the power on but you must be able to feel the back wheel slide. If your tyres and suspension are good you can gain a lot of time there. Accelerating from there I get into fifth before the fast right kink. You can get through there without braking, just snick it back to fourth but you have to work up to it, not for the first ten laps of the race.

"From there is the fastest part of the track, up into sixth along the straight. At the end there is a big, right hand hairpin. I brake late, very hard and change back to first. It is slippery but by the middle of the corner I accelerate. There is a short straight before the chicane. From third you go back to second. It's difficult, you have to turn in early for the left and try and get through the right flick quickly to accelerate hard through the last left onto the finish straight."

Patrick Fernandez

Ombu

Tobogan

Horquilla

© 1982 Motocourse

Autódromo Municipal de la Ciudad de Buenos Aires Avda General Paz y Avda Roca Buenos Aires ARGENTINA

Telephone No: 41 4839 Telex No: 18746

Circuit length: 2.48 miles/3.98 km

Nearest major town: Buenos Aires

Nearest international airport: Ezeiza, Buenos Aires

AUSTRIA – SALZBURGRING

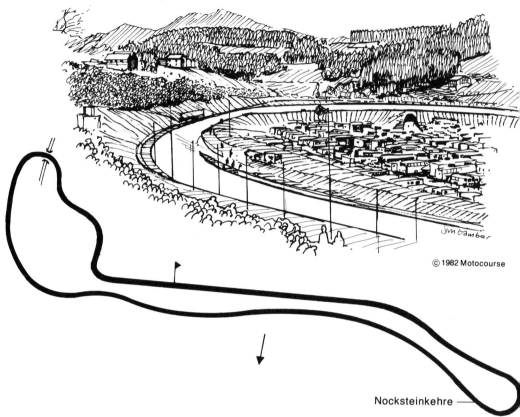

© 1982 Motocourse

Nocksteinkehre —

"It's a really exciting track, fast and I like it. I get into sixth on the 500 Kawasaki just before the right hander at the end of the straight and come out at peak revs, which is about 11,500. You exit the right hander in the middle of the track and aim for the apex of the left hand kink. Then you've got to get really hard on the brakes for the 180° loop; it's reasonably fast through there, though it is tight because of the banking. The surface is good and the track generally, and it doesn't seem to have got any bumpier since the first time I rode there in '73.

"I run round the loop in second, but you get good drive coming out and I hook it into third before I'm upright. Then you're into the superb, uphill climb which is really great, flat on the tank, curving left round the side of the hill, accelerating all the time into a flat out right hander. Then as you start to curve left for the next little left hander, you have to brake, trying to keep the bike well over to the left hand side of the road, knocking it back two gears for the important fast right hander behind the paddock.

"If you've got the gearing right, you can be on the power as the corner opens up and accelerating hard down the hill in fourth, revving to 11,000 before getting back on the brakes hard for the second gear, downhill right hand loop. It's another good corner and you've got to try and keep a tight exit line over on the

right for a good line through the chicane. I use second gear through the chicane, with the throttle backed right off, so you must keep the momentum going as you go through the left, and then get really hard over scraping your knee on the ground through the right, so that you can accelerate all the way through the left hander and onto the straight. It's difficult to set up the gearbox for the chicane and sometimes you want to be grabbing third as you go through the last left."

Kork Ballington

Salzburgring Interessens-Gemeinschaft
Münchner Bundesstr 9
A-5020 Salzburg
AUSTRIA

Telephone No: 33 6 01 10
Telex No: 63 35 85

Circuit length: 2.64 miles/4.24 km

Height above sea level: 2158 ft/658 metres

Nearest major town: Salzburg

Nearest international airport: Salzburg

BELGIUM – SPA FRANCORCHAMPS

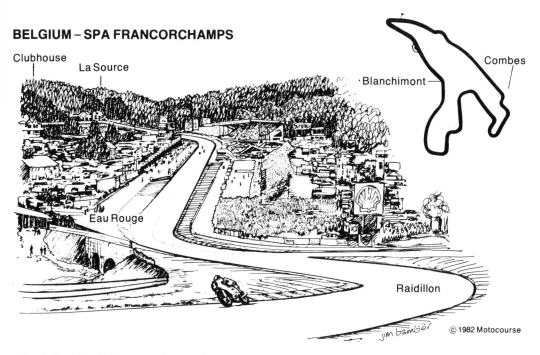

Clubhouse • La Source • Blanchimont • Combes • Eau Rouge • Raidillon

Jim bamber

© 1982 Motocourse

"For the first left and right corners there are about four different lines. Basically you can go in slow and come out fast if you don't have a quick machine and need a fast run up the hill. Or if you want to pass someone going in you can dive straight into the left meaning you have to make more of a corner of the right hander.

"Climbing up the hill I change into fourth early on the 500 Yamaha because the bike goes light over the brow on the next fast left hander causing the back end to step out. The track continues uphill through a bumpy, flat out right, no problem because there is so much room, to the fastest part depending on the wind direction.

"The next corner is the right and left onto the new circuit. It is the perfect place for late braking and I normally start past the 200 metre board. Changing down to second I prefer to go tight round the right hander giving me more room to accelerate through the left and perhaps blast past someone down the right hand side to the next right hander. It's a bit bumpy and down hill and I hold second all the way round the 180 degree corner and still in second get right back to the right hand side for the following left.

"This is the bumpiest corner on the track and leads to the fast downhill section. You are up into fifth gear before knocking it back to fourth and braking at about 100 metres for the double downhill right. The engine is doing about 8,000rpm on the over run as I run through the first left, drifting out to the curb on the outside then getting on the power and accelerating through the second left, making both corners one line.

"Hitting max revs in fourth on the way out, I touch the kerb and change into fifth. Peak in fifth at the end of the short straight and then you change back to second for the next right, left 'S'. It could be taken in third but second gives me better acceleration between the two corners. Get over to the right for the left hander and

accelerate through notching third before going back to second for the next right. There is a short straight to the right hander onto the old circuit which opens out as you accelerate through. On the power as you climb through the trees, changing up until I hit maximum revs in sixth through the fast left hand kink.

"Change back two gears and brake for the next, tighter left hander, and then wring its neck up to the silly 'bus stop' chicane. There is no overtaking through this section, you just have to queue up and go through in second gear. Get the exit right and accelerate round the left hander and down the straight to the hairpin.

"The hairpin is not really the place to outbrake anyone because you stand a good chance of losing going out what you have gained going in. You want to get round as quickly as you can to get the power on for the run down to the start and finish."

Steve Parrish

Circuit de Spa-Francorchamps
Route de l'Eau Rouge 280
4878 Francorchamps
BELGIUM

Telphone No: 087 2751 38
Telex No: 49271

Circuit length: 4.34 miles/6.98 km

Height above sea level: 1800 ft/550 metres

Nearest major town: Liège (Luik)

Nearest international airport: Bruxelles

161

CZECHOSLOVAKIA – BRNO

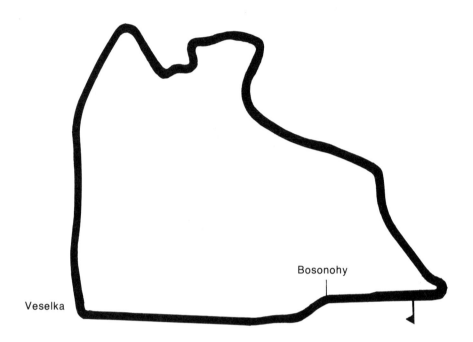

Bosonohy

Veselka

"Engine performance is very important because of the long uphill straight. From the start and finish you run downhill to the first village in fifth gear. There you brake for the first gear chicane which goes left then right. Through the village section there are four corners and the most important thing is to be fast through the last left. So I take the first right hander a little slow giving me a good line through the right left and the slight left going out of the village and downhill sixth gear straight to the next village.

"The next is a sharp, first gear, ninety degree corner. If you are brave you can brake at about 100 metres. There is a slip road to go straight on but if you get half way round the corner there is a house on the outside. From there a straight runs a little uphill before going down again; it is the second fastest part of the course. It ends at a first gear chicane, right and left, and from there you climb uphill through a series of eight bends starting with a big right hander through which you accelerate all the time, but the front wheel tends to slide away.

"The next is a second gear left and I hold second through the next right and left then into third for the next little left. Back to second for the next uphill right then through a left kink and a right kink accelerating through third and fourth.

"From there you are over the top of the hill and into the town section where the road suddenly widens. There is a very dirty right hand bend which is very slippery and

taken in second gear. From there you accelerate flat out through a fast fourth gear left hander and the track starts to go downhill through a very fast right. I hold fourth gear because it is another very slippery corner and there is no run off.

"Then it is flat out downhill in sixth at about 150mph (240kph) because I use Daytona gearing. Into the last corners I use all the track braking across the left hander up to the inside of the tighter right which leads back across the finish line."

Martin Wimmer

Grand Prix Brno
Automotoklub Brno
657 43 Brno
Basty 8
CZECHOSLOVAKIA

Telephone No: 27674

Circuit length: 6.79 miles/10.93 km

Nearest major town: Brno

Nearest international airport: Praha (Prague),
Wien (Vienna)

FINLAND – IMATRA

"Depending on the wind, the two straights give you about the same top speed. On the start and finish straight I get into top gear before the pits and I don't start braking until about 150 metres before the corner. I brake deep into the turn and then get the bike round the corner as quickly as possible so that I can be upright as I accelerate hard across the railway line. The bike always tries to wheelie because of the bumps there. Then the course goes into the right and left hander between the houses: it's one of the most difficult sections. There's a bump in the middle so you must be well over to the left hand side going in and turn early so that you can run across the bump straight. The left hander is equally tricky as there is a dip in the road. As you accelerate out the bike always goes up on the back wheel and it is difficult to keep it on the track.

"The next sharp right hander is a typical road circuit corner and I've watched the Dutch riders, who are used to riding on such tracks. They brake late, deep into the corner, turning in sharp and early to get the corner finished as soon as possible. Then they can pick the bike up and accelerate. It's important for your speed down the straight; this leads to a little, bumpy chicane. You turn off the track left, braking all the way up to the point where you flick it right and immediately accelerate through the left curve onto the road again. There are some ridges running along the road which make the back end slide as you go across them.

"The next right hander is a little wider and faster but the problem there is the wall of the house on the outside. You accelerate over the railway bridge and downhill to the next right, which makes the braking very tricky. It's quite a fast section and the temptation is to use the pavement on the exit which I used to do on the smaller bikes but with the 500 I stay on the road. You accelerate then down a short straight and brake through the slight left hander, keeping the brakes on as you peel right for the sharp bend. Then you must get yourself back all the way to the right hand side of the track to be able to accelerate early through the left back onto the start and finish straight."

Seppo Rossi

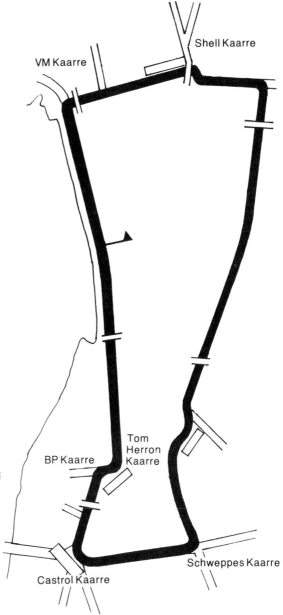

Imatran Moottorikerho RY
PI 14
55101 Imatra 10
FINLAND

Telephone No: 954 65656
Telex No: 121797

Circuit length: 3.08 miles/4.95 km

Height above sea level: 270 to 242 ft/63.11 to 73.86 metres

Nearest major town: Helsinki

Nearest international airport: Helsinki-Vantaa

FRANCE – PAUL RICARD

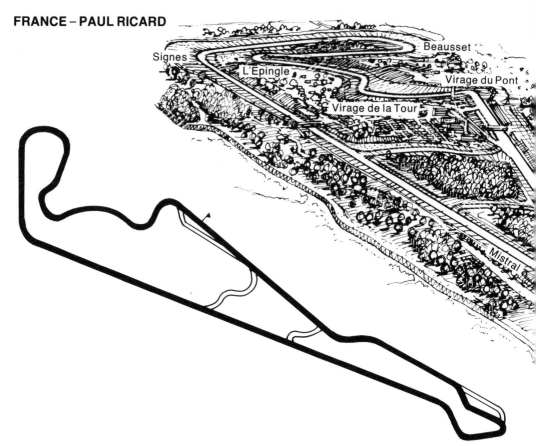

Signes
L'Epingle
Beausset
Virage du Pont
Virage de la Tour
Mistral

"I don't think Paul Ricard is a great circuit because it is a bit featureless, but it makes a reasonable Grand Prix track. One of the most exciting parts is the first left and right S bend which you take in fourth having knocked it back two gears from the start and finish straight. They are certainly corners for the brave. For the right hander you have to get it well leaned over and it's quite bumpy as you accelerate through and down the short straight to the chicane. This must be taken in first or second, a sharp right and left flick and a quick burst of acceleration to a tight, fairly ordinary right angled right. Then comes the more important right hander before the back straight, which you accelerate through in second, as it opens out, changing to third while still leaned to the right, before swinging it over to the left for the kink onto the straight. The line is critical there, and I work on reading the rev counter as I pass the end of the kerb on the right hand side. Every time I try to get more revs at that point as it makes such a lot of difference to the speed down the straight.

"The wind always seems to mess you around down the straight: it can change from lap to lap and gearing can be a bit of a gamble but it's one of the highest of the season. At the end of the straight is an ultra-fast right hander. I like fast corners, but not this one because it is very difficult to get the braking right, at 180 miles an hour you go a long way in a fraction of a second. At that speed I don't like to hold the brakes on too long into the corner so I release them as I peel off. I run through the corner in fourth, getting into fifth on the way out down the short straight to the long, long second gear loop. You can run in so fast, hitting an early apex going in and scrubbing off speed as it drifts out to the middle of the track. You hold onto the middle right to the end of the corner where you cut back across for a second apex. I reckon to be fairly good through there, making it all one line.

"Accelerating into third there's a very short straight before going back to second for a flip-flop right left. Then you must get well over to the right for a tight, 90° left hander which leads onto a long right hand corner through which I accelerate all the way. But you can't quite make it full bore on a 500: you have to ease off slightly as you hit peak revs in third, then accelerate again through fourth, holding the bike well over to the right to be on line to brake for a tight left hander. The braking and changing line from right to left all happens at the same time and when you get into the left you must again hug the inside. I never let it drift out more than a few feet from the kerb because you need to use all the road for the sharp, tricky right hander that leads back onto the start and finish straight."

Kork Ballington

ASA Paul Ricard
Route Nationale 8
F-83330 Le Beausset
FRANCE

Telephone No: 94 22 46 17
Telex No: 400988

Circuit length: 3.61 miles/ 5.81 km

Height above sea level: 2625 ft/800 metres

Nearest major town: Marseille

Nearest international airport: Marseille

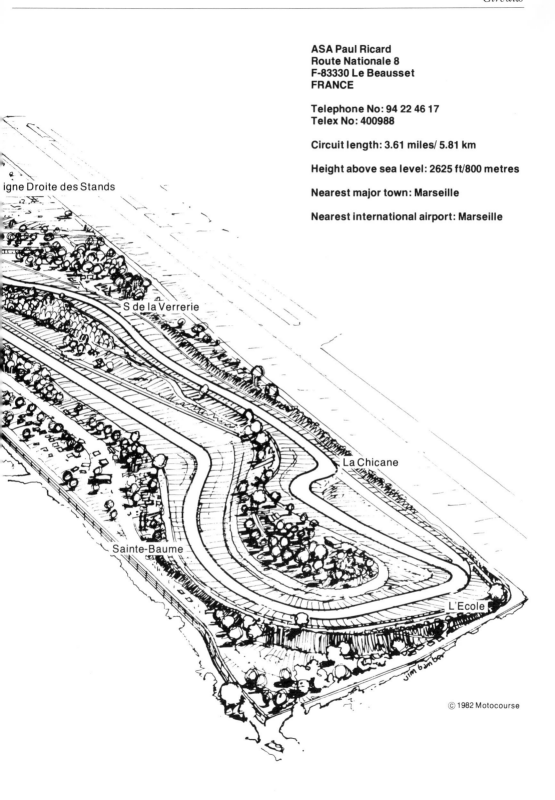

igne Droite des Stands

S de la Verrerie

La Chicane

Sainte-Baume

L'Ecole

© 1982 Motocourse

FRANCE – LE MANS – BUGATTI

"Along the start and finish I get into sixth gear on the 350 before the brow of the hill on the right hand curve. Cresting the rise the front wheel comes up, but not fiercely. Down to the first hairpin I brake very late for the first right hand hairpin. It is difficult to judge because of the downhill approach.

"It is very slippery and you must know the correct line because it is not obvious. I brake in very deep then turn quickly and get the bike upright as soon as I can to accelerate out. Accelerating away from the first gear hairpin I get into fourth before braking and changing back to third for the next left. It is another tricky corner, a very long left.

"I prefer to brake all the way in on the inside and hold the bike on the inside all the way round. Using all the track coming out, I accelerate and get into fifth gear going downhill to the next first gear, double right hand corner. There is one simple line but you have to be careful because the exit is slippery.

"Along the next straight you get into fifth or perhaps sixth depending on the wind before the left hand kink. This is flat out on a 250 but on a 350 you must roll it back a fraction. It is a difficult corner and a bad entry will put you on the grass coming out because it runs off camber.

"You then have to work hard to get the bike across to the left for the next corner, a second gear right. Don't use all the track through there so you can get into third and go through the left hander. Out of that you must get hard on the brakes and back across the road to the left for the tight right leading back to the finish. As you accelerate out of there be careful of the white lines on the outside of the track."

Jean-François Baldé

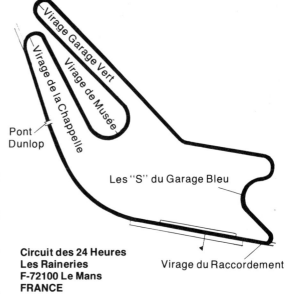

Circuit des 24 Heures
Les Raineries
F-72100 Le Mans
FRANCE

Telephone No: 43 725025
Telex No: 720637

Circuit length: 2.64 miles/4.24 km

Height above sea level: 184 ft/56 metres

Nearest major town: Le Mans

Nearest international airport: Paris-Orly

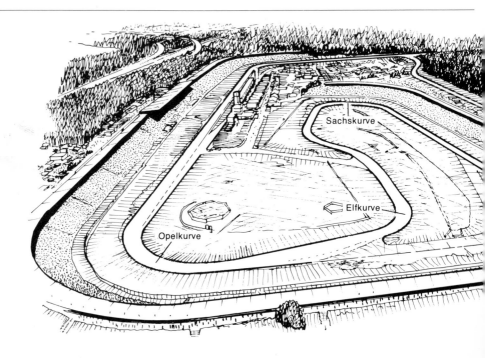

GERMANY – HOCKENHEIM

"It's another one of my favourite circuits. I love the long, fast blast through the trees to the first chicane, and then from there to the big right hander. The track surface is quite grippy in the dry, but in the rain the stadium infield is really bad because of all the tyre testing that is done there.

"Across the start and finish line you are in fourth, and at the end of the straight are either peaking in fourth or have just got into fifth when you have to change back down to second and brake for a nondescript, 90° right hand corner. That brings you onto the first long straight and out into the forest where people are forever seizing because of the tremendous amount of oxygen given out by the trees.

"The chicanes are quite fast and are taken in third gear. You brake while leaning right, right up to the apex, and then just flick it left, then accelerate, curving right again, out onto the straight which is really a slight curve. You accelerate all the way and just get into sixth before knocking it back a couple of cogs for a really great right hander. It has an even radius and as soon as you get onto the inside line you must accelerate as smooth and as steady as possible all the way onto the next straight.

"The run to the second chicane is just as fast as the first and this time you brake as you curve left off the straight and then flick it right. These are how chicanes should be made because they do slow down the top speeds but they are still quite fast and skillful, unlike the Mickey Mouse chicanes at Imola. After the second chicane there is another straight that runs back towards the stadium and during a Grand Prix you can't help but see the huge crowds in the grandstands and it creates a tremendous

atmosphere. It's a difficult right hand corner into the stadium, taken in third gear, and for some reason I never seem to get through there as smoothly as I'd like.

"Then there is a short straight before you change back to second for a 180° left hander that is quite well cambered. Accelerating from there the track rises slightly through a little left and right, where you have to roll the throttle back a little on the 500 as it shakes its head. The last double right is difficult and important. It's taken in one line: the first corner you are right on the limit with your knee on the deck, and the second half is tighter so while you're still leaned hard over you've got to ease on the front brake a bit to lose some speed. If you get it right, you'll be accelerating right out to the track's edge down the start and finish straight."

Kork Ballington

Hockenheim-Ring GmbH
D-6832 Hockenheim
(Motodrom)
WEST GERMANY

Telephone No: 06205 7021
Telex No: 465984

Circuit length: 4.22 miles/6.79 km

Nearest major town: Heidelberg

Nearest international airport: Frankfurt

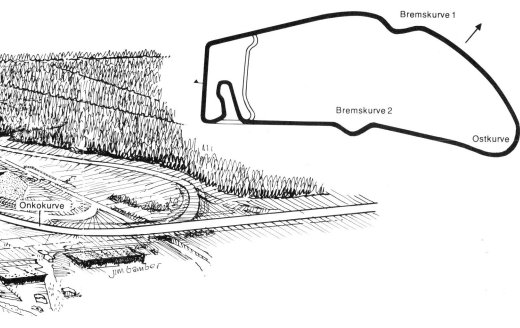

Bremskurve 1

Bremskurve 2

Ostkurve

Onkokurve

jim bamber

© 1982 Motocourse

167

GERMANY – NÜRBURGRING

Marco Lucchinelli on the three cylinder NS500.

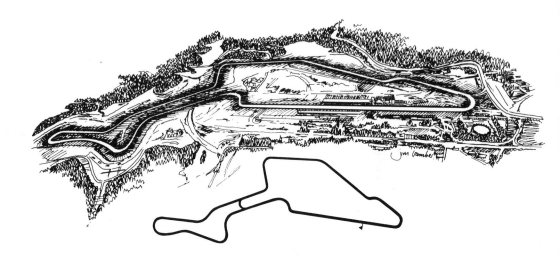

"From the start of a race the first corner is very important because there is only one fast line. The right hander is a second gear corner that is quite fast if you are on that one fast line and then the following left hander opens out and if you use the full width of the track you can accelerate all the way through it sliding out to the curb.

"As I exit the left hander I change into third and then top fourth before the fast sweeping left hander which is taken in fourth and there are two lines on the approach to the next tighter right. Both can give you about the same lap time so you should bear them in mind. If you go fast round the left hander and use all the road you will arrive at the right up the inside of the corner which is good for overtaking even if you are not as fast out of that right hander and down the hill.

"Braking earlier gives the normal wide line to the right hander and a fast exit from the second gear corner down the hill where you get into fifth before the 180 degree Dunlop bend. Again there are two possible lines here and I prefer to brake up the inside on the right and take a tight line and accelerate hard back up the hill. That is a second gear corner again and on the 250 you can almost accelerate flat out through the next left but not quite. Because you are going up hill rolling back the throttle into the left slows you too much so I prefer to ease the throttle back a fraction mid-way between the two corners and then accelerate flat through the bend.

"You are into fifth gear and the next left looks tight but again it is second gear and you have to choose second gear carefully at the Nürburgring because all the second

gear corners are slightly different and you have to make it work everywhere. Here the revs are a little low but you accelerate to the next right hander and get third right on the exit. The following right hand kink is flat out even in the wet but then the bike does slide around a bit but speed through there is important because it leads to the fastest section of the course and maximum speed is achieved just before braking for the last left and right chicane. If you are leading into there you can normally win the race but you must not make a mistake at the last corner which would usually be taken with a wide line going in but if you are trying to stop someone getting past you can brake up the inside and take the tight line and accelerate out onto the start and finish straight."

Martin Wimmer

**Nürburgring GmbH
D-5489 Nürburg/
Eifel
WEST GERMANY**

**Telephone No: 02691 2031
Telex No: 086 3919**

Circuit length: 2.82 miles/4.542 km

Height above sea level:

Nearest major town: Koblenz

Nearest international airport: Köln-Wahn & Bonn

GREAT BRITAIN – DONINGTON PARK

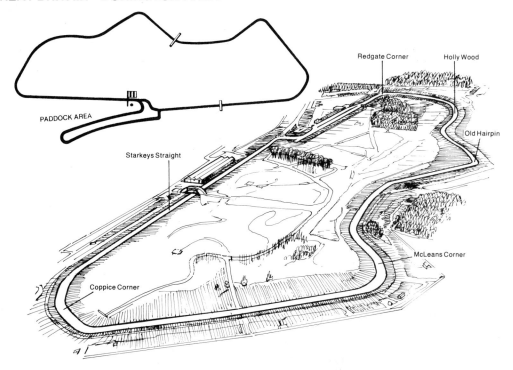

Donington Park

"On the 250 I'm in third gear past the start and finish and just get into fifth before braking for the first right hander, diving in early, changing back three gears with the brakes on all the way into the corner. I use the inside line because it is a good line for overtaking even if others on a wider line might get the power on a bit earlier. I use all the road on the way out, accelerating through third.

"Going into the next downhill right I get over to the right hand side early and hold it there accelerating all the way, short changing through fourth and fifth to stop the rear wheel sliding while I'm cranked over.

"I keep it flat as I pick the bike up and peel off for the left, you can't see the apex until you have started to turn. Through the left I let the bike run out to the right and only get it three quarters of the way back to the left for the next right hander.

"Brake, and change back two gears to third for the right which is faster than it looks. There is a dip in the corner and you must wait for that before gassing it, using all the road on the way out. From there you accelerate all the way through the left hander changing through fourth to fifth past the old bridge. You use all the road going into the left so that you can get a good line into the right hander. Sometimes I change into sixth but usually hold fifth, straight lining the exit from the left straight up the inside of the right braking late.

"Round the corner in second gear over the rough patches, the camber seems to run away a bit. From there you accelerate, getting into fourth before knocking it back to third as you brake for the next right. The

approach is up a rise that hides the corner and you just have to know where to peel off. I get as close as I can to the first apex then get on the gas as I come back for the second apex and then drift out to the edge of the track with the back tyre sliding.

"I change through fifth to sixth just under the bridge flat out before braking for the chicane at between 150 and 100 yards, depending how brave I'm feeling.

"Hold the brakes on all the way into the way into the right hander changing to second and accelerate through the left to the start and finish."

Jeff Sayle

Donington Park Racing Ltd
Castle Donington
Derby
DE7 2RP

Telephone No: 0332 810048
Telex No: 377793

Circuit length: 2.5 miles/4.02 km

Height above sea level: 310 ft/94.5 metres

Nearest major town: Derby

Nearest international airport: East Midlands

Sheene chases Spencer.

GREAT BRITAIN – BRANDS HATCH

"It is flat out in top across the start and finish line on the 500. I brake for the first right hander just as I go past the Lucas sign. The track dips down before rising again, making the bike go light. The apex is out of sight over the hill until the last second then you throw the bike over and go steady on the throttle until you've crossed the bump.

"Just before the bottom of the dip I change up into fourth and hold that gear all the way up the hill to the next right. Brake as late as possible. Down the centre of the road because if you don't someone will pass you up the inside. It's a long corner and you have to hold the bike down as you accelerate, keeping it on the inside strip of tarmac because the outside is slippery. You feed the throttle on nice and gentle, using about three quarters of the road on the way out and accelerate down the hill changing to third and pulling the bike back towards the right of the track for the left hander.

"I get to within about three yards of the right hand kerb before peeling off into the downhill left. I snick it up into fourth before the apex. The early change takes the edge off the power but I keep accelerating all the way out to the white line. Hold fourth all the way to the next which goes round a long way. It looks as though you have gone past the corner before it is time to peel over. By using a late apex you can get the bike almost straight before it goes light over the top of the hill.

"The bike wheelies in all the gears as you accelerate over the top and down the dip. The bike is flat out before you get to the superb big right hander at the end of the straight. Back to fourth gear if you are going well or third if you hesitate. Brake hard and late then tip it in real hard.

"Accelerating all the way out to the white line I hold fourth until half way down the next straight then grab fifth before changing back to third for a bumpy right hander. It's smooth enough going in but the middle and exit are bumpy. Hitting the kerb on the exit puts the front wheel in the air and down the dip you get fourth and then fifth. The suspension bottoms in the dip as you hit the apex of the right hand kink and then up the rise to the next 90 degree right. You can't see the apex, you wait as late as possible then tip it in with the power on in third.

"I hold third down the short straight, over revving it and hauling the bike over to the right for the left hander. Brake and change to second for this slightly banked left. The rear wheel wobbles as you drift out to the white line. Down the next straight I get into fifth before braking for the last right. Back into fourth and lean the bike in. There about four different lines but you must have a feel for sliding your bike. I make an early apex and then drift out under acceleration before coming back to the second apex at the beginning of the pit wall. I am flat on the stop in fifth by the second apex and snick it into sixth as I drift out to the line."

Keith Huewen

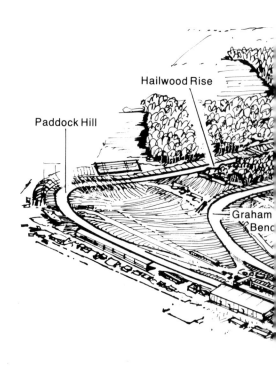

Hailwood Rise

Paddock Hill

Graham Bend

Brands Hatch Circuit Ltd
Fawkham
Dartford
Kent DA3 8NG

Telephone No: 0474 872331
Telex No: 96172

Circuit length: 2.61 miles/4.21 km

Nearest major town: London

Nearest international airport: London Gatwick

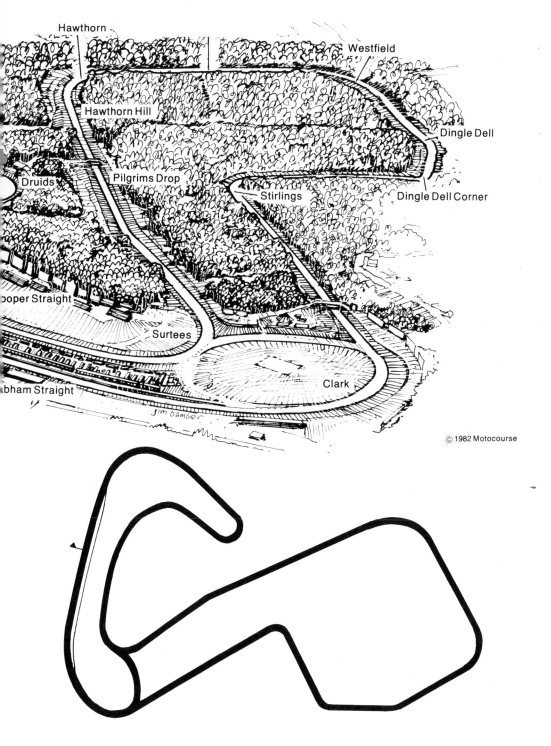

Hawthorn

Westfield

Hawthorn Hill

Dingle Dell

Druids

Pilgrims Drop

Stirlings

Dingle Dell Corner

oper Straight

Surtees

bham Straight

Clark

Jim Bamber

© 1982 Motocourse

GREAT BRITAIN – SILVERSTONE

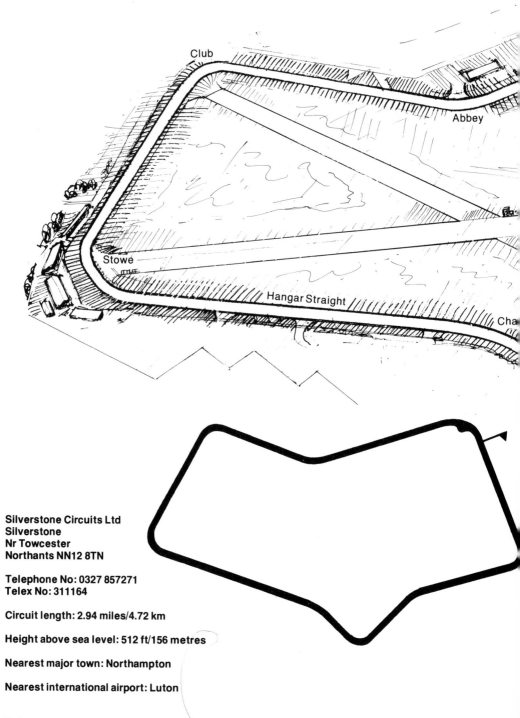

**Silverstone Circuits Ltd
Silverstone
Nr Towcester
Northants NN12 8TN**

**Telephone No: 0327 857271
Telex No: 311164**

Circuit length: 2.94 miles/4.72 km

Height above sea level: 512 ft/156 metres

Nearest major town: Northampton

Nearest international airport: Luton

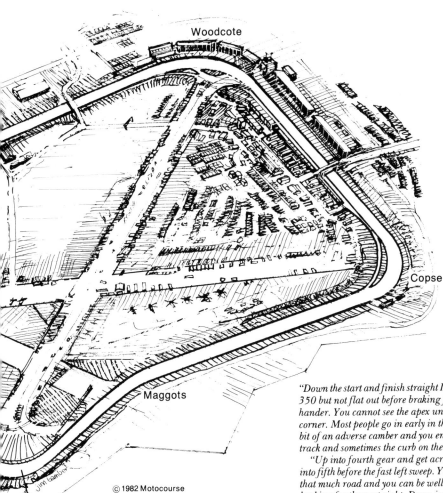

Woodcote

Copse

Maggots

© 1982 Motocourse

Jim Gambet

Becketts

"Down the start and finish straight I get into fifth on the 350 but not flat out before braking for the first right hander. You cannot see the apex until you arrive at the corner. Most people go in early in third gear, there is a bit of an adverse camber and you end up using all the track and sometimes the curb on the way out.

"Up into fourth gear and get across to the right and into fifth before the fast left sweep. You don't have to use that much road and you can be well over to the left for braking for the next right. Down into second for the slowest corner on the track. As soon as you get out of the right, get your knees and arms tucked away to run flat out through the left hander and onto the straight.

"Flat out down the long straight, I change back three gears as I brake at the end for the right hander. There is a bump about three quarters of the way round but then you drive out hard holding a reasonably tight line. I get into fifth down the next straight before going back to third for the right hander.

"There is a tendancy to go in too early but it's best to turn in late and get a good drive out for the run up the hill. Accelerating through fourth I just change into fifth as I peel off into the fast uphill left, still flat on the tank with knees tucked in. I hold fifth until I've crested the rise or the engine dies a bit. The bike is flat out in sixth before I brake and change down to third for the last right. You have to hold it in tight or you loose too much ground on the way out. There are some bumps about three feet out from the curb. It is best to go inside them, if you run across them the back end steps out spoiling your drive across the finish line."

Graeme McGregor

175

GREAT BRITAIN – ISLE OF MAN TT MOUNTAIN COURSE

"The secret of going fast round the TT circuit is knowing exactly what place to be in at precisely the right time. Through the 140 and 150 mile an hour sections you cannot afford to be a foot off line. If you are a foot off line or a few degrees wrong in direction the speed accentuates it so much that you will end up miles out. Then you will have to roll it off and that will spoil your speed for the next mile.

"One problem with learning the circuit it that it is so long that you tend to forget the mistake you made on one lap by the time you come round to do it again. You have such a lot to think about in between that you might peel off too late again and again until after 20 or 30 fast laps things like that should stick.

"The thing is that you have no time to think about what has just happened and the line you should have taken you have to always be concentrating on what lies ahead and where you should be on the road or you will mess up the next section. There is a lot of difference between being fast round the circuit and being very fast.

"I have got beyond the stage of looking at targets, the 100mph lap, the 110mph lap. I am now looking for every second. It means that I cannot afford to take it easy round the slow corners and concentrate on certain sections, I have to be going fast everywhere.

"Racing in the Isle of Man relies a lot on concentration and putting yourself in the right mental state to tackle the course. If you want to win you have to ride very quickly, to do that you have to push the thoughts of danger to the back of your mind but not forget them completely.

"Before the race I am probably most frightened of the fact that once on the bike I might forget about the dangers. I have to remind myself where I am all the time."

Jon Ekerold

Promoted by:
The Auto-Cycle Union
Millbuck House
Corporation Street
Rugby CV21 2DN

Telephone No: 0788 70332
Telex No: 311156

Course length: 37.73 miles/60.70 km

Nearest major town: Douglas

Nearest international airport: Isle of Man – via Manchester

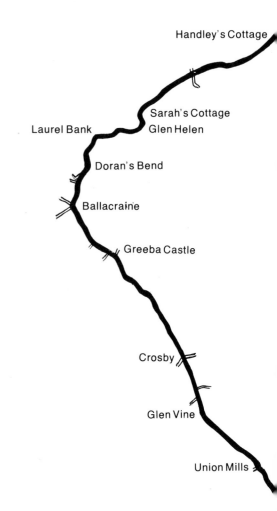

Handley's Cottage

Sarah's Cottage
Laurel Bank   Glen Helen

Doran's Bend

Ballacraine

Greeba Castle

Crosby

Glen Vine

Union Mills

Braddan Bridge

Quarter Bridge

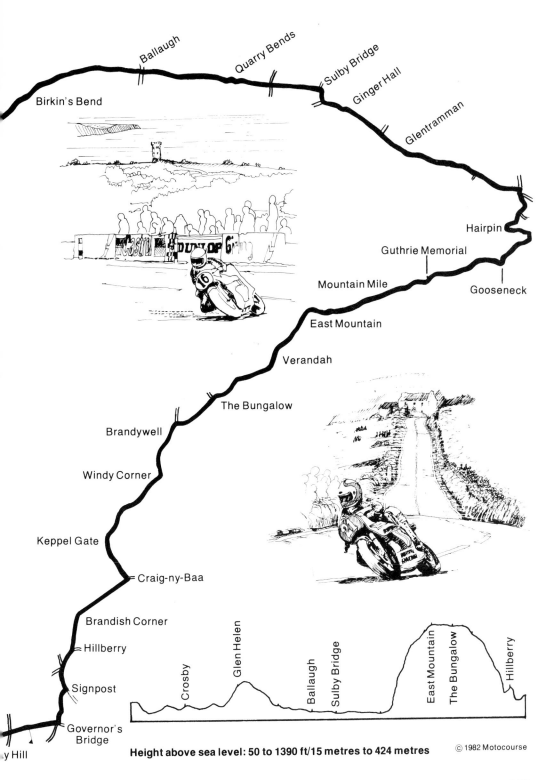

Ballaugh

Quarry Bends

Sulby Bridge

Birkin's Bend

Ginger Hall

Glentramman

Hairpin

Guthrie Memorial

Gooseneck

Mountain Mile

East Mountain

Verandah

The Bungalow

Brandywell

Windy Corner

Keppel Gate

Craig-ny-Baa

Brandish Corner

Hillberry

Signpost

Governor's
Bridge

y Hill

Crosby

Glen Helen

Ballaugh

Sulby Bridge

East Mountain

The Bungalow

Hillberry

Height above sea level: 50 to 1390 ft/15 metres to 424 metres

© 1982 Motocourse

177

HOLLAND – CIRCUIT VAN DRENTHE

"I really like the layout of the track and it is fairly safe but it is way way too narrow for today's bikes and passing back markers is just about impossible.

"You go through the right and left kink after the pits flat and get into sixth just as you go under the bridge. The braking for the first right hander is not as hard as it used to be on the old circuit with the longer straight and tight first gear corner. Now it is down to second as you brake for the right hander and then accelerate up to fourth before the left hand kink in the new section of track.

"Half way round the kink you have to get on the brakes and then it is real hard to get the bike back across to the left hand side of the track to make the second gear right hander. I really like that turn and then you are on the gas again accelerating up to fourth gear going white line to white line through a series of curves to the next tight right which again is down to second.

"The fourth gear run back towards the pits is tricky because the last right hander before the long, long left can suck you in too fast and if you don't watch out you can be running out of road.

"The long, long left is another second gear turn and the exit is important because you want to try and get through the next series of corners flat. I can just about do it but it takes every inch of road and all my strength changing to third before the right hander and fourth between that and the left.

"There is quite a left hand kink before the next right which is the tightest corner on the circuit and takes some very hard braking. The next section is banked corners which are second gear but faster than they look and they lead to the very tricky third gear right hander going back towards the start and finish where you have to use every inch of road. The next two lefts are taken as one changing back to fourth from fifth and not using a lot of throttle but you are still going very fast with a lot of momentum. Then it is hard on the gas before braking for the chicane which is very slippery and out onto the start and finish.

Eddie Lawson

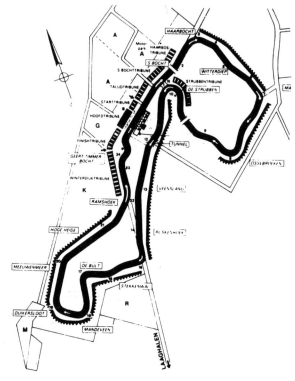

Stichting Circuit van Drenthe
Postbus 150
9400 AD Assen
HOLLAND

Telephone No: 05920 55000
Telex No: 53821

Circuit length: 3.81 miles/6.13 km

Height above sea level: 33 ft/10 metres

Nearest major town: Assen

Nearest international airport: Eelde (Groningen)

ITALY – MISANO (SANTA MONICA)

"The track needs a bike with bottom, mid and top end power. It is also bumpy so most machines need a lot of work to make them handle. The track was resurfaced in 1982 but all they did was resurface the bumps and make the track slippery.

"At the end of the start and finish straight there is a left kink into a right hander. I go into the left hard on the brakes, straight lining it almost up to the right hander. Then flick it over and accelerate; the track opens up through a right curve and I change getting into fourth and then fifth going over to the right hand side before braking hard for the tight left.

"Down into second, the tight left leads to progressively faster lefts and you accelerate all the time, third, fourth,

fifth through the last left kink and into sixth down the fast back straight. It's not a long straight at that speed and soon you're hard on the brakes for the left hand hairpin at the end.

"I change down to second and it's a long corner that brings you right back on yourself. You accelerate through a slight right kink and down a short straight before hooking it back a gear and braking for a tight right. From there there is another short straight to a double left that is quite tricky. The second part is tighter and that leads into a slight right kink onto the start and finish."

Barry Sheene

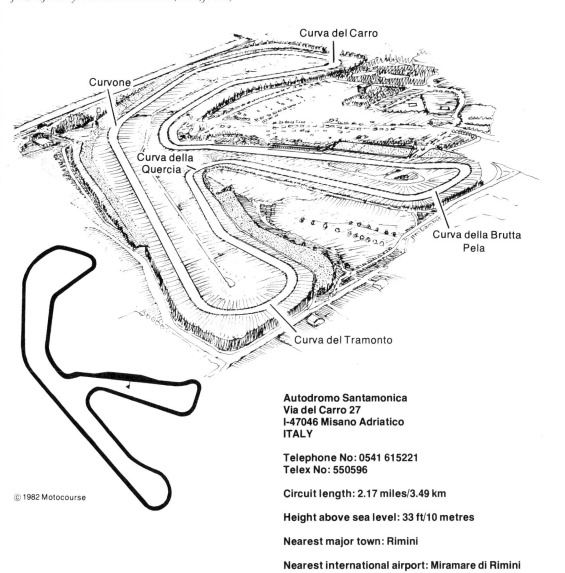

Curva del Carro

Curvone

Curva della Quercia

Curva della Brutta Pela

Curva del Tramonto

© 1982 Motocourse

Autodromo Santamonica
Via del Carro 27
I-47046 Misano Adriatico
ITALY

Telephone No: 0541 615221
Telex No: 550596

Circuit length: 2.17 miles/3.49 km

Height above sea level: 33 ft/10 metres

Nearest major town: Rimini

Nearest international airport: Miramare di Rimini

179

ITALY – IMOLA

"The first corner, a left hander, is really two, accelerating all the way on the 250 I let it drift out through the first ready to come back and make more of the second part. I change into sixth and getting back across to the left for the next right hander. I go flat out down on the tank through the right, trying to keep the bike over to the right to be lined up for the tight left hander.

"Straighten up and get hard on the brakes, changing down to second. Round the left accelerating as the track rises out of the turn, through third and fourth, over to the left for the right kink over the top of the hill. Then it's hard on the brakes and back to third for the left hander.

"The track keeps going left as you accelerate downhill to the first of the awful chicanes that have spoilt the track. Hard on the brakes and down to first turn right, left then up into second for the last late apex right and accelerate up the hill. Into third then through a left kink, stay over to the left hand side of the track to the second chicane which I get through in second if everything is spot on. Right, left then a short squirt to a left, right. From there the track goes left as you get over to the right for the run down the hill to the ninety degree left. Hard on the brakes and back to second. From there I drag second to the next left accelerating through and hitting third on the way out.

"I hold third from there, rolling the throttle back for the fast right left chicane then a burst of acceleration, grabbing fourth before going back to second for the last left and right onto the start finish straight. It is a track with good traction but it was an awful lot better before they put in the chicanes."

Richard Schlachter

Curva de Tamburello

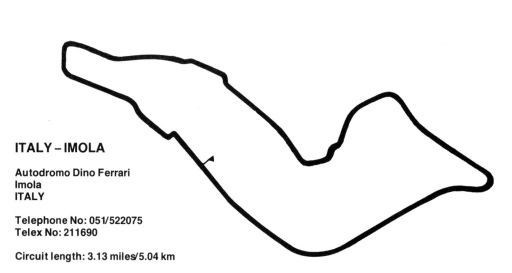

ITALY – IMOLA

**Autodromo Dino Ferrari
Imola
ITALY**

**Telephone No: 051/522075
Telex No: 211690**

Circuit length: 3.13 miles/5.04 km

Height above sea level:

Nearest major town: Bologna

Nearest international airport: Bologna

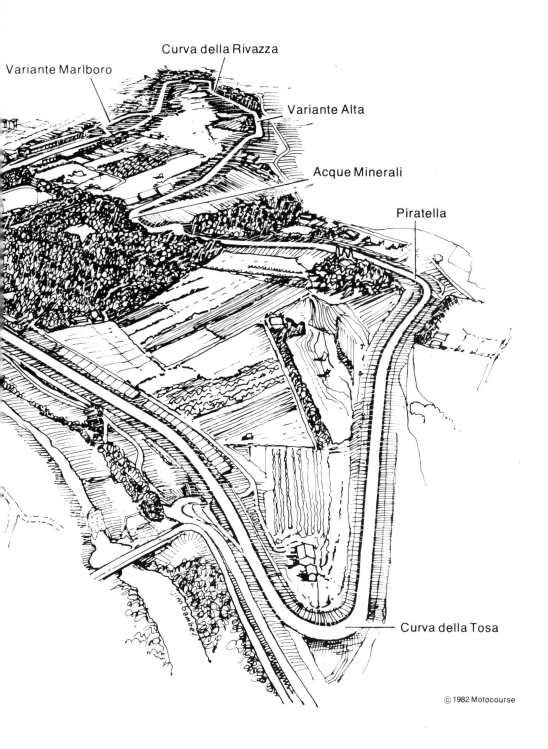

Curva della Rivazza

Variante Marlboro

Variante Alta

Acque Minerali

Piratella

Curva della Tosa

© 1982 Motocourse

ITALY – MONZA

"Riding at Monza was a disappointment for me because it is one of the great old circuits but now it is shabby and decaying. The fast main straight runs straight into one of the awful chicanes.

"I use a high first gear and a sixteen inch wheel is a definite advantage to get through the tight left, right, left, right. No one can ever pass, you just have to get your braking right, touch all the kerbs as you go through and make sure you get the exit right.

"You accelerate all the way through the following fast right up to the next chicane. This one just goes left and right and then you accelerate to the double right. I use third gear for both which are distinctly separate corners.

"Get a good line through the second right for the fast run down the dip, accelerating through the left kink into top before braking for another double chicane. This is slightly more open and taken in second gear, left, right, left. I snick it into third on the second left and use the curb on the way out.

"From there it is a fast blast down the straight changing into fifth before braking and changing to third for the last long right, the Parabolica. It is tight at first but you accelerate as the second part opens out and it's a real test of rear tyres. I change into fourth while still cranked well over using all the road over to the barrier and drifting onto the old circuit as I get onto the straight."

Steve Parrish

Autodromo Nazionale di Monza
20052 Monza
Parco
ITALY

Telephone No: 039 329866
Telex No: 316434

Circuit length: 3.60 miles/5.80 km

Height above sea level:

Nearest major town: Milan

Nearest international airport: Milan

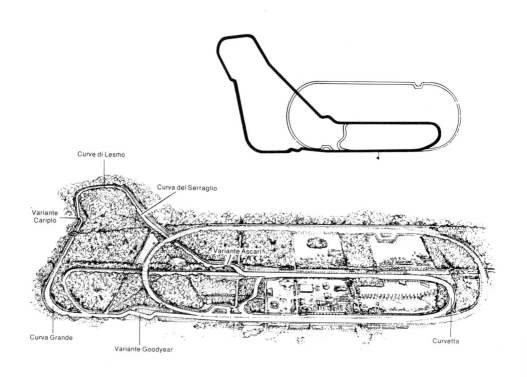

Curve di Lesmo

Curva del Serraglio

Variante Cariplo

Variante Ascari

Curva Grande

Variante Goodyear

Curvetta

ITALY – MUGELLO

"I get into sixth gear after the end of the pits before the flat out left hander over the rise. The line is not too important but the bike goes light so that you must not grab the brakes as suddenly as you normally would but squeeze them on and wait till the weight comes on the front before giving full pressure.

"You want to make a late apex to the tight first gear right hander because the drive out is important. It goes uphill and you mustn't let the bike run wild otherwise you will spoil the line for the next left. Because the track is running uphill, the front is trying to come up and slide out but you must hold it in and I get into second before the next left and right.

"You must get a tight line through the first left so that you can drive out through the right then on the exit the slight banking to the corner goes away before you have finished turning and that causes the back to slide. Then it is up into third before the next left and right to second going in.

"Again the first left is important because you need to accelerate through the right for good speed, down the following straight and there are some ripples on the exit of the right hander.

"Into third up the straight I clog it back to second for the next right. I could go through in third but the track starts to run downhill so I use second just to hold the bike back a little and you have to watch it or you can lose the front end through this right hander. Heading down through the left you can get on the power quite early because there is a lot of room on the way out. You go through the next fast right hander in third as the track begins to go uphill again and you keep the power on hard but watch for the bump right in the middle of the corner. Because the corner turns uphill you get pushed into the road and there is more grip than you think. In the same way though the next fast right can catch you out because you begin to go over the top of the hill and the back end can wheelspin and slide.

"Out of the second right still in third the track begins to run downhill again and you have to watch the braking for the next second gear right and left because it can trick you into going too fast and then if you just pitch it in you will lose the front end.

"Out along the next straight the engine revs out in third before the long, long right that comes right back on itself and begins to run downhill. I get third before the next left and you can go in fast and accelerate through with the back wheel spinning on the way out of the right hander.

"For the last long downhill left, you brake in a straight line from fourth and then you have to watch it as you turn in bcause there are driving lines between the strips of tarmac which run all through the corner and the front tries to tuck under you as you go across them.

"I use second going in and then third before half way and put the power on hard. You have to watch for a different patch of tarmac that starts the bike weaving but otherwise it is hard acceleration out onto the start and finish straight again."

Ron Haslam

Autodromo Internazionale del Mugello
Viale Amendola 36
I-Firenze
ITALY

Telephone No: 055 846351
Telex No: 571203

Circuit length: 3.26 miles/5.245 km

Nearest major town: Firenze

Nearest international airport: Firenze (Florence)

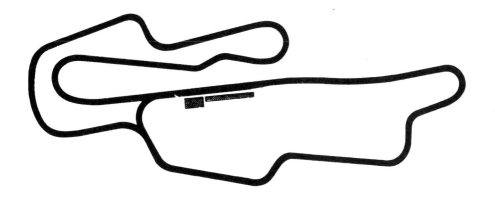

SOUTH AFRICA – KYALAMI

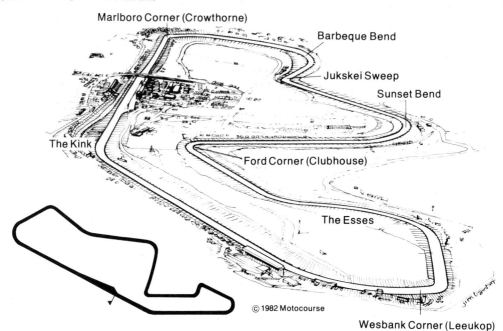

Marlboro Corner (Crowthorne)

Barbeque Bend

Jukskei Sweep

Sunset Bend

The Kink

Ford Corner (Clubhouse)

The Esses

© 1982 Motocourse

Wesbank Corner (Leeukop)

"The main straight at Kyalami is long and fast with a down hill drop at the end; I think the gearing would be about the same as the Salzburgring, one of the fastest Grand Prix circuits. Kyalami is six thousand feet up, so jetting is obviously very different from sea level.

"At the end of the straight is a tight, right hand corner almost 180° which I used to take in second when I raced 250 Yamahas there several years ago. You need to use a braking marker at the end of the straight. I used to use the lines marking the changes in the tarmac but since the track was re-surfaced for the car Grand Prix in '82, that has changed. You can't go very fast around the right hander but it does open up in the exit as it drops away down the hill. You accelerate through third to fourth but you have to roll it off slightly through the very fast downhill right hander. I used to hold it hard on the inside, away from the bumps, so as to be well over to the right for the next left. If you can't hold a tight line you've got to get out three feet because there's a series of ripples all the way through the corner.

"If you're over to the right, the next left is flat out and you can either hook it into fifth going in, or hold it in fourth, and either way it's a tremendous feeling cresting the rise through the left hander. You use all the road as you approach the next right flat out in fifth. The next right is tricky because the approach is fast, you can't see round the corner and it seems to slope away. You have to peel off early, hold a tight inside line in third gear, accelerating as you see the exit. Get back into fourth as you haul the bike hard over to the right hand side before braking and changing down to second for the next tight left.

"You can get a hard burst of acceleration down the short straight to the Esses, getting into fourth before

hooking it back a gear and peeling off late into the left hander. You must keep in to the left because the road drops away off camber. Then by the time you've leaned over for the right hander, you can accelerate hard through the dip, getting back into fourth on your way up the hill to the last, tight right.

"Because the corner has an uphill approach you can brake late, curving in from the left hand side of the road early. You peel off for the corner from the middle of the road and then hold it tight on the inside. You accelerate hard and let it drift out as you crest the rise onto the main straight. Just before the start and finish there is a wide, fast, right hand kink that is absolutely flat on a 250 and although it would be more difficult on a 500, I still think it would be full bore."

Alan North

Kyalami Grand Prix Circuit
PO Box 4961
SOUTH AFRICA

Telephone No: 702 1677
Telex No: 424104

Circuit length: 2.55 miles/4.10 km

Height above sea level: 5500 ft/1676 metres

Nearest major town: Johannesburg

Nearest international airport: Jan Smuts

SPAIN – JARAMA

"On the 250 I get into sixth just past the start and finish. I gear the bike mostly for the corners so I might be slightly over revving before the first right hander. It is two bends taken almost as one. You brake late and hard changing back to second. Off the brakes a bit after the first early apex and let it run out before coming back and accelerating through the second.

"Up through fourth before the right hand kink then just feather it a second and drive through. Keep it leaned over to bring it back for the next left and brake hard changing back to second. I take a late apex which means I only use three quarters of the track and can get three quarters of the way back across for the next 180 degree right.

"Down to first gear for this which is also a late apex and grab second on the way out. Pull the bike back across to the right, roll it back a hair then gas it through the left and up the hill. You use all the road and the back wriggles as you go over the top. Up into fourth gear through the right kink and then hard on the brakes for the next double right, late apex again.

"Accelerating down the hill you get third and then fourth before you lean into the left kink. The front end chatters through there and you hold fourth down to the sharp left hander. Braking hard for the left hander I pull the bike over slightly for the right because there is a slight kink in the track then into first and lean hard over.

"As you get on the power there is a small bump that makes the back end step out but I keep accelerating through second to third over the hill to another double right. Hard on the brakes and back to second hitting both apexes. From there I get into fourth and just feather it a second before driving through the last fast downhill right. Use all the road out to the curb and then flat out to the finish line."

Richard Schlachter

Circuito Permanente del Jarama
c/o Real Automovil Club de Espana
José Abascal 10
E-Madrid 3
SPAIN

Telephone No: 447 32 00
Telex No: 45411

Circuit length: 2.06 miles/3.31 km

Height above sea level: 1640 ft/500 metres

Nearest major town: Madrid

Nearest international airport: Madrid

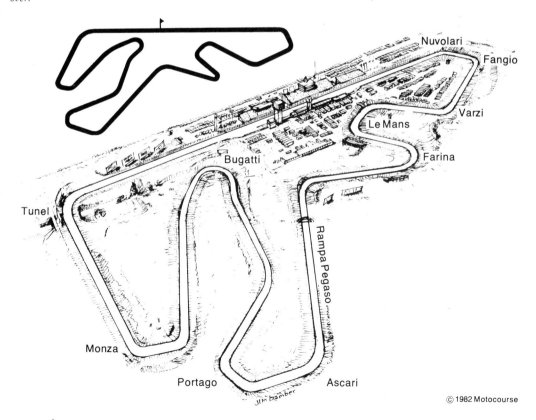

© 1982 Motocourse

185

SWEDEN – ANDERSTORP

Graeme Crosby combines a great personality with a wealth of riding talent.

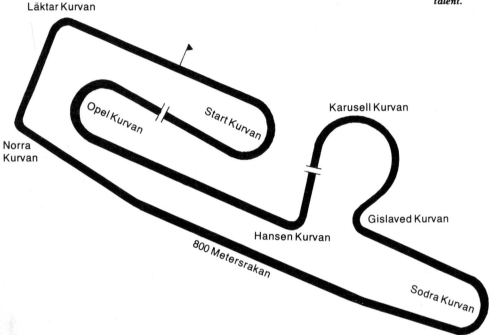

"I liked the track more before the last corner at the end of the back straight was changed. The surface is not too bad but the grass is overgrown and untidy. The first corner after the start and finish is important: it's a long corner and Tepi Länsivuori told me to brake all the way into it. As soon as you leave off the brakes you get back on the power but you are leaning well over and if you are not careful you can find yourself going too fast at the end. From there it's a short straight to an equally geometrical 180° left hander. It's the same kind of corner, but with perhaps a bit more banking to keep the speed up. Then there's another short straight to a sharp 90° left, which is a good place for passing people on the brakes, and up a short straight to a long right hander which is more than 180°. You can go in very fast at the beginning, scrubbing off speed, so that you are slower in the middle, and then accelerate coming out. That's a little bit tricky as there are some small bumps at the end. You must be careful to keep the bike well over to the right, though, because you have to brake immediately for the tight left. If somebody is chasing you, you must let the bike run over a little more to the left to stop him passing you on the brakes, accelerating out of the corner you can use the kerb as banking.

"It's another short straight which give you very little time to see the signals from the pits before the double right which is taken as one corner. You often go into this too fast and slide out wide, but you should hold a tight

line so you can accelerate hard out onto the straight. The main back straight is actually a light aircraft runway and is very wide. It makes it difficult to judge the braking point at the end as there is a sudden reduction in width running up to the tight right hander. Then there is another short straight to the last right which is the only really bumpy corner on the circuit. A lot of people fall off there and there is very little run off, but at least it's not very fast."

Seppo Rossi

Scandinavian Raceway
PO Box 180
S-330 20 Anderstorp
SWEDEN

Telephone No: 0371 16170
Telex No: 70327

Circuit length: 2.51 miles/4.03 km

Nearest major town: Göteborg

Nearest international airport: Göteborg

USA – DAYTONA

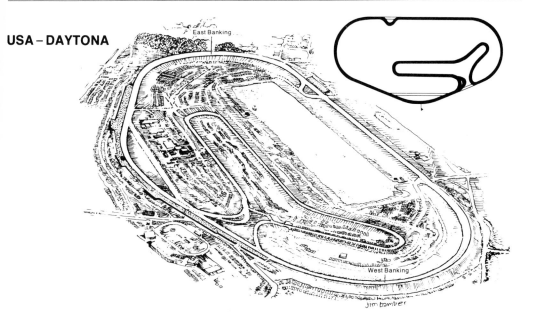

East Banking

West Banking

jim bomber

"It's one of my favourite circuits. You'd think it was pretty simple: the turns are all flat and you can see them a long way away, but it's a lot harder than it looks.

"With the new track layout behind the pits the line round turn one has changed and you have to apex it late and not drift out too wide or you cannot get back to the left for the following right and left. Turn one is taken in second and you change into third and on the V four just back off a fraction to get the bike to change direction into the right hander. Then it is flat through the left.

"The next 180 degree right is a second gear turn which opens out so you have to get a late apex which will let you get on the power early. You have to time your acceleration so that you are pointing in the right direction to use all the road on the exit but not run out of it. I get into fourth on the 500 before the left hander and just change back to third and drive through and down to the next 180 degree right hander which is just about the slowest point on the race track.

"You brake hard and really throw it over; the corner seems to tighten up on the exit so you have to wait a bit before accelerating. The next left, turn five, in some ways is the most difficult at Daytona. There's one bump that's impossible to miss and if you get your suspension to work there it won't anywhere else on the track. All you can do is apex late because if you apex early and accelerate across the bump you stand a good chance of losing the back end.

"From the apex you accelerate right up onto the bowl. You want to get right up onto the top of the banking. From there I start to gradually drop down until about three-quarters of the way around when I drive hard down off the banking, just getting into sixth, as I drop onto the back straight.

"The chicane is deceiving because it is flat. People brake too early. I brake late and turn in late. I'm on the brakes all the way through the left right up until the

point that I flick right. I get the bike turned through the right as soon as possible; I want to be on the throttle at the first hay bale of the right hander. I aim for the centre of the left side of the chicane, just missing the hay bales, doing as little movement on the way out as possible. I am actually slow through the right hander, but am soon upright and accelerating hard up to the top of the banking again. If I have to sling shot somebody, I'll drop back a fraction and wait so that I am running in on them as they begin to drop down. Then you can get a maximum pull to throw you past. There's no doubt, though, that Daytona is a horsepower track and you've got to have a fast motor cycle to get results."

Freddie Spencer

Daytona International Speedway
Drawer S
Daytona Beach
Fla 32015
UNITED STATES OF AMERICA

Telephone No: 094 253 6711
Telex No: 564353

Circuit length: 3.84 miles/6.18 km

Height above sea level: 5 ft/1.5 metres

Nearest major town: Orlando

Nearest international airport: Orlando

Left and right, through the corkscrew at Laguna Seca.

YUGOSLAVIA – RIJEKA

"It's a long way to go to get to Rijeka but when you get there it's not a bad track. You have to have a machine that handles well, particularly you must be able to change direction quickly because a lot of the corners run straight after each other.

"Across the start and finish line I am flat out in sixth gear, lining the bike up for the first right hander. I change down into third and brake all the way through the right hander, straight into the tighter left. I go down another gear and make sure I get a good line out of the left hander so that I can accelerate around the following right. That corner opens up so I accelerate all the way through, changing to third and then fourth, and by the time you get through the right you are going quite fast and have to get on the brakes hard for the next second gear left. It's a long corner more than 180° and it brings you onto a short straight leading to a tricky section that goes left, right and then left. You have to get through the left on a good line so that you can be fast through the following right and left. Then there is another short burst of acceleration to a left hander which is off camber, and you have to brake hard through the left for the following tighter right. Once through there, there is another left, right and left which are all hard work heaving the bike from one side to another and the track goes uphill onto the back straight. You have to get the last left lined up well as it affects the speed down the straight.

"It's actually a long curve rather than a straight but by the time you get to the end you are going hard in fifth and I brake deep into the last left hander. It's a long, long corner with two apexes, and I make sure that I get the second apex just right to line me up for a fast run through the right hand kink and back onto the start and finish straight."

Barry Sheene

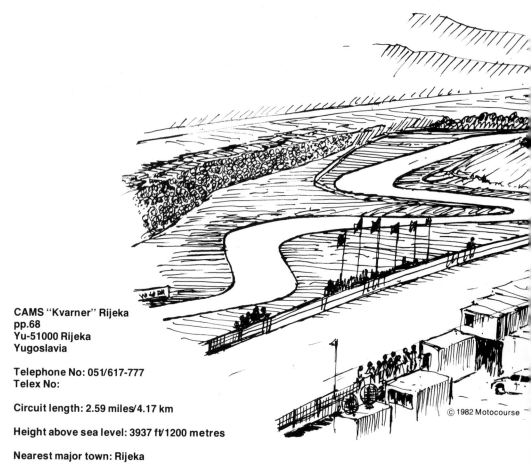

CAMS "Kvarner" Rijeka
pp.68
Yu-51000 Rijeka
Yugoslavia

Telephone No: 051/617-777
Telex No:

Circuit length: 2.59 miles/4.17 km

Height above sea level: 3937 ft/1200 metres

Nearest major town: Rijeka

Nearest international airport: Trieste

© 1982 Motocourse

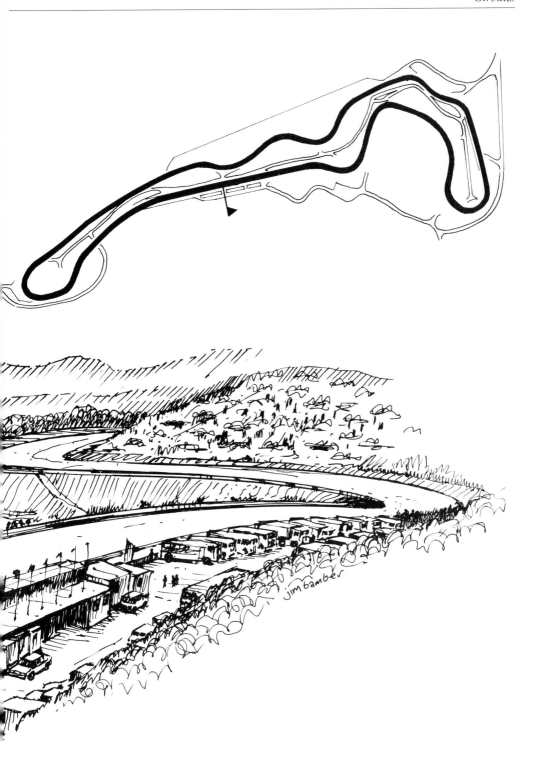

jim bamber

8
Riding

Yamaha owners' manuals that accompany their TZ road racers give the rider specific instructions as to how he should conduct himself. "The rider must mould his body forward and crouch down behind the cowling so that air resistance is minimised. A good start is a dominant factor in winning races."

Even before the rider steps aboard his machine at the start of a race the manual tells him to take exercise. "The rider must be in good physical shape before the race he must warm up his body by taking light exercise."

There is little doubt that in their production racers, the TZ range, Yamaha have for many years provided excellent machinery for the privateer but there is obviously far more to winning races on their machine than following the instructions in the manual.

The professional riders at the top of their sport have spent a large proportion of their learning life developing their riding skills. More than most conventional careers, an exciting sport like motor cycle racing invokes an enthusiasm and a desire to learn that makes the rider dedicate all his waking hours and intelligence to going faster. Anything less than total dedication will result in a second class racer and no amount of natural talent will alter that. There are just too many skilled competitors and only an exceptional effort can bear fruit.

The years of learning required to make a world champion create an incredible store of knowledge. It is a knowledge that most riders find hard to impart to others. They spend so long turning over split second actions on the race track inside their own heads that they have no method of passing on the information to anyone else. When you go to school to learn mathematics or science you are taught by someone who stands in front of the class and imparts that knowledge to you. You read about it in books and then you write about it yourself. It is natural to talk about such subjects and you are taught the language, the equations and the examples that best explain things to someone else.

But motor cycle racing is rarely taught, even racing schools only

go through the basics and a few short sessions cannot hope to convey years of concentrated learning. There is no established language to convey the exact feeling that the handlebars give as the front wheel begins to slide and turn in, the timing required to gently ease on the throttle so that the rear wheel begins to slide in harmony and the weight is transferred from the front to back wheel, the front wheel being hauled into the inside of the corner by the pull of the chain.

World Champions have learnt how to cope with that and a thousand other situations on their own, out on the track at a hundred miles an hour in the split second that separates completing the corner from crashing hard into the ground or trackside obstacle. They have had no particular reason to pass on what they have learnt to the people who might understand what they are saying, other riders, because they are, after all, competitors. Most riders do not consider it knowledge that can be passed on, it is contained within them as something they do without conscious thought. Something in the subconscious cannot readily be put into words.

There are fortunately some facets of riding skills more obvious

to the observer that the rider has been asked about often and that happens in more than a fraction of a second. Passing, braking, cornering and slipstreaming, etc. all require learning and developing to the point where the rider can commit himself to each action absolutely positively almost without thought, often leaving his mind free to think several stages ahead, of the next corner or the next rider to be passed.

Watch a riders eyes, either in a photograph or reality and you will see that his gaze is far ahead of his position on the circuit. It is most noticeable on tight corners where he will be looking across the corner to the exit point while he is still braking and heading for the apex. In that position he has already committed himself to a certain line into the corner, decided when he will finally release the brakes

Riding in the wet demands delicate use of brakes and throttle.

and apply the throttle, has registered the patch of dust-covered oil that demands a fractional delay in acceleration and may create a short slide from the rear that he must not confuse with a total loss of traction.

Information is being absorbed by the rider from many sources. His eyes tell him about the road ahead, the condition of the track surface, the riders in front and any flag signals being shown. The rate of change of his view tells the speed at which he is travelling. His hands feel the response of the handlebars, they sense the way the tyre is gripping the road; it might be pattering or sliding. If the forks are twisting the feel will be different. Somewhere between his feet and his backside the rider must be able to sense the grip of the rear tyre and suspension action. His sense of balance supplies information about the angle of lean, weighing gravity against centrifugal acceleration (see chapter 2, page 37) and he must know if the front of the machine is dipping or rising. His ears pass on details of the engine activity as do his eyes if he has time to look at the rev counter.

This information is constantly changing and the rider's realisation of his own position and that of the machine must keep pace with every fractional alteration. Not only must the rider know that but he must always be making exactly the right corrections through his hands, feet and body weight to guide the machine perfectly and respond to any emergency. The more he learns about the way the machine responds to certain inputs and acts in certain circumstances the quicker he can respond to information and the more able he is to avoid possible disaster.

There is a lot to be learnt about the basics as well as the fine riding skills that almost have to be learnt the hard way, by individual experience. Information about the basics can be conveyed by the spoken and written word, to a point at least. As always, those who excel at their chosen occupation, those who are brilliant and confident in their own ability will answer any reasonable question you might ask because they are already considering the answers to questions you will never think of asking.

Ask Graeme Crosby for instance about his lightning push starts that so often put him into the first corner at the head of the pack. "It takes practice and you must have the bike carburated exactly right so that it will fire easily. I just take two steps and release the clutch, I lean on the machine to stop the rear tyre slipping as I release the clutch. Because I take only two steps and most people take four I can hear my engine start. When it fires I pull in the clutch again without moving the throttle. Then as the revs rise I open the throttle as I leap aboard and let out the clutch."

Imatra in Finland was the last of the true road circuits to be used for a 500 Grand Prix. Like other Dutch riders Jack Middelburg was used to the varying surfaces and trackside obstacles; sadly he was killed on a road circuit in Holland early in 1984.

While the fastest line through the corner usually starts at the outside of the track, a favourite overtaking manoeuvre is to rush up the inside and push your way in.

Practice can be a big help with starting and getting off the line at the head of the field and is very important particularly at club level where the races are so short. The late Dave Potter made his name originally riding a modified production Norton Commando in club events which were often six lap dashes. He was tremendously successful and attributed a good proportion of it to his starting procedure. "The Commando had to be started in neutral for the production race kick starts. I practised and practised until I could fire up the engine with one swinging kick and then hook the engine into gear with my foot as it came up from the bottom of the swing. It was all one movement and very fast but I had to get it right first time or there I was in gear with a dead engine."

Once you have the motor cycle started and under way the racing starts in earnest. Jon Ekerold has his own theory about how hard to ride from the start: "I say that if you're going to crash then do it on the first corner, because then you haven't put a lot of effort in and worn out the motor for nothing. But seriously, I like to go fast from the start so that I get into a fast rhythm. If I pussyfoot around I find it difficult to get going later on."

First corners are always tricky, dangerous places with so many riders fighting for the same piece of road. Fall down in the middle of the pack and you're likely to be hit by following machinery. If you want to make headway from the tail of the field at the first corner, you will have to go round the outside. The safest place is probably on the inside so that you can squeeze into the traffic jam just before the apex of the corner. Riding round the outside requires more bravado, especially on cold tyres, but if you do fall down most likely you will be on your own. Taking the wide line does raise the significant possibility that you will be pushed off the tarmac at the exit of the corner.

At hairpins, riders often do not use the classic racing line but enter the corner nearer the middle of the track, leaving less room on the inside for others to overtake.

There is a lot to be said for taking it easy for the first few laps, waiting for the tyres to warm up and for the traffic to thin out. When Barry Sheene won his two World Championships in 1976 and 1977 he did exactly that, never clearing off from the start, but riding round somewhere in the top ten, feeling out the opposition and making sure the machine was 100% before forcing his way into the lead.

No-one has so dominated the 500cc class since that era and as Graeme Crosby pointed out, Grand Prix races are hard work right from the start. "Strategy is something you play if you can't win the race by sheer speed. In Grands Prix you've got to go flat out right

One of the real thinking riders, Martin Wimmer, on his 250 Yamaha.

*Downhill corners
are always
difficult because
it is not easy to
accelerate all the
way through
them and the
front wheel tends
to slide away.*

from the start and if you want to be World Champion you've got to do that in every race. You can't sit back and wait for the opposition to drop out as maybe you can in a longer race like Daytona's 200 Miler. When you are Grand Prix racing you've got to be with the leaders right from the start because there are usually four or five who break away."

Grand Prix races are rarely, though, won at faster speeds than are set up during practice. This suggests that the riders can go faster than they actually do and there are several reasons for this. One is the sheer length of a Grand Prix, some 45 minutes, and the physical exertion and concentration required to put in a really fast lap cannot be maintained over that period. Riders also find that their tyres deteriorate in performance when pushed hard and while this is acceptable for one practice lap it is best to ensure that the tyres last the distance.

Tactics, then, do play a part because although the rider is racing flat out the top speed to which he restricts himself is a fraction below the maximum capability of the frame, suspension and tyres. This can produce some tremendously close racing as no rider is prepared to break away, pushing himself and the tyres to the limit with the risk that he cannot maintain that pace for the race distance. In this way, tactical races do evolve and in some respects close racing is self propagating because riders on slightly slower machinery can slipstream faster riders.

Slipstreaming (see chapter 2) uses the wake that a speeding motor cycle makes in the air to suck along a following machine. The distance behind the leading motor cycle that the slipstream can be felt depends on the speed of that machine and the properties of its streamlining. As a general rule, at speeds near or above 100 miles (160km) an hour, the slipstream will be felt while the leading bike is still some twelve feet (four metres) ahead but it is not until you close to within three or four feet (one metre) that you are completely within the slipstreaming envelope. As the top speeds of the fastest 500s exceed 170mph (275kph) this distance is lengthened somewhat to around five feet (1.52m).

It is clear that at that speed with so short a distance between the motor cycles there is little time to take avoiding action if the leading machine slows suddenly with engine failure. Experienced riders tell of the small puff of smoke given out by two strokes just before seizure that can act as a warning by a fraction of a second of imminent disaster. If the bike you are following does not have high level pipes, though, you do not even have that slim chance of escape as it is not possible to see the lower half of the machine in front when crouched down behind the fairing. Kork Ballington describes his method of self preservation: "When I am slip-streaming somebody I don't run exactly in their wheel tracks but slightly out to one side. I still get a good tow and it does give half a chance if something goes wrong. It also makes it easier to see the road ahead and gives a better view of the next corner and the braking point. That is critical because you must know precisely where you are when you get to the end of the straight. If he sits up and brakes while you're still flat on the tank, you'll run into the back of him. Time it so that you just move over to one side as he brakes and if things go according to plan you can leave your braking a yard or so later and go past."

More than just using slipstreaming to keep up with the machine in front, it can be used to overtake if your engine has different power characteristics. Maybe you have poor mid range but high top end, in which case there is the chance of a tow through the weak spot, pulling out to pass when your bike gets into full song. Even with precisely equal machines, the added momentum gained by being sucked up behind the machine may give enough speed to at least pull alongside, if not actually to go past. You can also use a slipstream to change up earlier enabling you to pass as the leading rider changes gear because as he does so his engine will drop away from its maximum power rpm.

At a circuit like Daytona, where high speeds are maintained for long distances, slipstreaming is all-important. Dale Singleton has won twice there and knows how to use it to his advantage. "When you're on the banking you have to draught a bit to the high side using the pull to drag you up on the banking so that you can drop down and pass on the low side."

If it is impossible to pass on the straight using the slipstreaming technique or the machine's superior speed, then you must look for somewhere else, and more passing is done under braking than anywhere else. One of the greatest exponents of heavy, late braking in recent years has been Gregg Hansford as his greatest rival, Kork Ballington, points out: "Gregg brought short circuit scratching to Grand Prix racing and when we first met in the 250cc and 350cc classes it took me a while to get used to it. He was especially brilliant on the brakes and at the first Grand Prix where we were both riding the works Kawasakis I couldn't get anywhere near him. That was in Venezuela. At the next race in Spain I finished nearly a minute behind him and by the time we got to Italy which was the fifth Grand Prix I beat him in both the 250 and 350 races. It was just a case of working up to it but nobody was better on the brakes than he was."

Late braking requires perfect timing: if you are braking on the limit then you cannot afford to miss the braking by a foot because if that happens you will go into the corner too fast and, at the very least, run wide. It is generally recognised that it is necessary to use some sort of braking marker when slowing dramatically from high speed as at the end of a long straight or for a tight hairpin. It is the easiest way to get consistently accurate braking. Some riders use braking markers at a lot of corners while others, like Barry Sheene, take the opposite view. "I prefer not to use a braking marker but to get a picture of the corner in my mind and when I arrive at the point where I know that the picture is right, then I brake."

For road circuits, like the Isle of Man, Dundrod and the North West 200, peeling off points are also vital. This is because with the corners obscured by walls and hedges the line of the track cannot be seen as you approach. When racing at high speed there is no chance to alter your line halfway through the corner and you must choose a reference point at which to peel off that will put you on the right line to get through the corner safely. Because road circuits are always lined with trees, walls, etc. there are usually plenty of markers to use for both peeling off and braking.

Overtaking under braking has the advantage that it is not even necessary to be faster than the other man through the corner. By braking late enough to draw alongside him, on the inside, you can force him to go wide. Or even better slip in front, stealing his line so that even if you are going too fast to make a neat job of the corner he must slow and tag along behind. Beware, of course, for in attempting such a manoeuvre it is all too easy to lose the front wheel, braking deep into the turn which will likely cause both of you to crash. Passing on the inside of a corner means that you have to complete a shorter distance than the rider who takes a wider line. The time difference is more significant the tighter the corner. It is purely a case of simple mathematics: if, for arguments' sake, we assume that the lines taken by the two machines must be separated by a gap of three feet (one metre) we can consider two corners, one with an inside racing line forty feet in diameter, a typical hairpin, and another faster corner 120 feet across. In turning through 180°, taking the inside line of the tight corner the rider will travel 62.8 feet. The rider cornering three feet on the outside completes a 46 foot diameter turn and travels 72.3 feet, a difference of 9.5 feet (3 metres).

The difference in distance travelled for the 120 feet corner is the same, 9.5 feet (3 metres) as you can check by calculating πd[1]. The crucial difference though is that the speed around the tighter

---

1 πd is the Formula for the circumference of a circle and this is divided by two as the racing line around a hairpin approximates a semi-circle.

corner is probably half that of the speed around the 120 feet corner so that riding around the outside of the former will lose twice as much time as it will through the wider, faster turn. And it is lap times that count. This theory is born out in practice and you will rarely see a rider successfully pass another around the outside of a tight hairpin.

The line through one corner is often affected by the line from the previous one and a rider must make up his mind as to which corner is more important and must take precedence.

For this reason riders braking for a hairpin will often use the centre of the road, inviting another rider to try and make it around the outside and giving him less room on the inside. Seeing another rider come up the inside, the leader may well move over, pushing him further towards the inside and making him brake harder. If he does not, the inside rider will be forced to overshoot the corner.

Such manoeuvres require perfect judgement and even the very

best of riders occasionally get it wrong as Kenny Roberts admits: "Once I rammed Randy going into the Mallory Park hairpin. Obviously I didn't mean to, but he moved over and took a different line and I hit his back wheel. We both stayed on and he looked round at me as if to say 'What the hell do you think you're doing?' and 'If you want it that bad you can go first'. I just shrugged my shoulders and we got back to racing. We had a good laugh about it afterwards, but there are some people you try not to go anywhere near. Not so much in Grand Prix racing but at International races the local guys are out to prove something and they'll do anything to get past. You've got to give them plenty of room, especially on the brakes, and hope that you can get away from them around the fast corners."

Although a lot of passing is done under braking, most riders are happier when they can get the power on, feeling the machine more under their control when accelerating. If the front tyre slides going into the corner there is little time to save it as the wheel immediately turns in and slides away completely. With the power on the rear may slide but if you believe Randy Mamola, that is no cause for concern. "When you're accelerating you can feel if the back tyre starts to break loose. Then you just hold the throttle steady until the tyre catches again. The worst thing possible to do is to back off suddenly because the tyre digs in and flicks you over the high side. If you keep the throttle steady, there's no way you're going to fall down."

It sounds very simple coming from someone like Mamola who does it all the time but going a stage further there has often been talk of the top riders power sliding through corners in a moderated speedway style, with the back tyre a foot out of line with the front. Jon Ekerold describes this idea as rubbish: "Consciously drifting the bike I don't understand. For me, when the back end breaks away I'm on my ear. I just don't believe it's possible. Sure, you get a bit of sideways movement but not consciously drifting. Either I've still got to learn to ride a motor cycle or some people talk a lot of hot air."

In wet weather both braking and acceleration must be treated much more delicately. The tyres offer less grip and once they lose adhesion it is even harder to recover than in dry conditions. Weight transfer means that braking hard in a straight line is still possible as the front tyre is pushed through the water film. Once you start to lean into the corner, though, braking should largely have finished because the front tyre will slide easily.

Under acceleration the rear may slide, but at least this is controllable especially as the sudden re-gripping that occurs in the

Pit signals are important, especially for races of Grand Prix distance. They tell the rider his position in the race and often how far he is behind the man in front. A board showing 4−3 indicates that he is in fourth place, three seconds behind the rider in front. 1 +2 will show that he is leading by two seconds.

dry leading to high siding, does not happen in the wet. Acceleration must be gentle though and even in a straight line wheel spin is common.

It has often been suggested that American riders are able to control a sliding motor cycle because of their dirt track racing experience. Roberts disagrees: "I don't think that riding a dirt tracker teaches you anything very much that you can't learn on a road racer, but I think I learnt to be more aggressive and determined because of dirt track racing in the States. When you've sat on the start line on your Yamaha among eighteen other guys on Harleys, and all the Harley fans in the crowd are throwing beer cans at you, then that teaches you to go fast."

Doubtless an important part of going fast is determination, but confidence is also a major factor. "When you go into a corner really quick, and it seems so easy you wonder what the other guys are doing", says Ekerold. "If you've got to try and go quickly, then forget it, just slow down to the point where you know what you're doing and build up to it. Self confidence is the thing. When you're on top you can do amazing things and get away with it."

Not only must the rider be confident and determined, but if the race is Grand Prix distance maintaining concentration can be a problem. Riders vary a great deal in this respect. Barry Sheene, for instance, does not worry about concentration as such. "Once the race settles down into a pattern, and perhaps I'm following another rider who I've ridden with often before, my mind quite often wanders. I might think about what I've done with the car keys or about flying the helicopter. But if something goes wrong you never miss it. So I suppose I've been concentrating all the time but when you're riding fast everything seems to happen in slow motion. Your brain's working quickly and you've got plenty of time to brake and

Apart from everything else, riders must be looking out for flag signals which warn of oil on the track or an accident. A stationary yellow flag indicates danger, exercise caution and when waved means great danger, be prepared to stop. A red and yellow striped flag denotes oil on the circuit and when both are held up together, the race has been stopped prematurely, and the same thing can be indicated by a red flag. A white flag shows than an ambulance is on the track. A black flag accompanied by a riding number tells that rider that he must stop. A blue flag is sometimes used to indicate that another competitor is trying to overtake.

turn. It's only when something goes wrong, perhaps a rider you are about to lap moves onto your line, that you suddenly realize how damn fast you're going. Then you can get a fright for a minute before you settle back down to a rhythm again. Anyway, every few laps I stop thinking about other things and concentrate on how the race is going, check my pit boards and decide whether it's time to speed up, pass the guy in front, or whatever."

Kork Ballington, on the other hand, says that while he is racing his concentration never strays: "I always force myself to maintain 100% concentration. It's too easy to make silly mistakes if my mind wanders. That's why, when I was riding the 250 and 350 Kawasakis I sometimes won by such a long way. Even if I was out in front it was safer to ride nearly flat out because it kept my concentration up. That's why I'm probably not so good in practice: there isn't the determination and concentration that racing brings and I can't ride as fast. I think if an incident happens or something goes wrong in practice I'm probably slower to react."

Randy Mamola makes a concerted effort to keep himself on his guard: "I smack myself when I'm riding if I find myself losing concentration. If a rider like Kenny comes past it has one of two effects: it either turns my determination down or it really makes me more determined. If you see a rider in front going at a steady speed then you can normally boost yourself 5% to catch him."

Catching the rider in front is what the race is all about and when it comes to the last laps everyone will be trying to find a way to do it. "When you're following someone, you've got to find a weak link in their riding", says Graeme Crosby. "You find which part of the track you're faster and then work out how you're going to use it to get past. You've got to try that manouevre several times without actually doing it. But that can always go wrong because the bloke goes flat out on the last lap and you end up in the dirt for trying."

Jon Ekerold prefers to be in front at the start of the last lap. "I like to be in the lead because the hardest part is getting past. After racing with somebody for the whole Grand Prix you know where he's going to make his big effort and you should be able to stop him doing it."

Although to state the obvious winning races is what it is all about, winning championships means more than any one individual result. It is World Champions who can temper the aggression and determination that normally makes them race winners to accept a lesser position if the need arises. Twelve points for a second place are better than falling off on the last corner and consistency so often pays dividends in the end.

9

Practice makes Perfect

For Irish closed road race meetings like Tandragee 100 and
Cookstown 100 there is no such thing as practice. All the riders get
is two warm-up laps before being brought round to the grid for the
start of the race. If the jetting or gearing is wrong, or the rider is not
familiar with the circuit, hard luck. He will have to do the best he
can.

At the other end of the scale, the Japanese works teams have
their own factory test tracks and test riders who develop the
machines before they are brought to Europe. The same teams then
hire the circuits for a couple of days prior to a Grand Prix, allowing
the works riders time to set up the suspension, carburation, test
tyres and learn the track if need be. Every Grand Prix then has at
least two days of official practice before race day. All that track time
allows a lot of testing and development but there can never be too
much.

Before any serious testing can be done, the rider has to learn the
circuit. Each rider has his own way of doing this: if the circuit is
short enough he may walk round it, perhaps with another rider
who knows the track well and who will point out the lines, braking
points, the apex of each corner,[1] surface irregularities, bumps and
slippery patches, places for overtaking where different lines can be
used when necessary and so on. For longer circuits a bicycle or
mini-bike is more reasonable and for exceptional cases like the Isle
of Man TT course special methods may give an advantage. Most
riders go round the course in a car or on a motor cycle and it has
even been suggested that the TT course can be learnt best at night
as the headlamps of the vehicle pick out only the road straight
ahead, avoiding distractions and replicating the tunnel vision that
riders experience when racing.

In his first year of Grand Prix racing, 1982, Freddie Spencer had
a lot of new circuits to learn. "I don't worry about how fast I'm
going when I'm learning a new circuit. The braking points seem to

1   The point at which the rider comes closest to the inside kerb of the corner is known as the
    apex.

212

come naturally to me, mainly I'm just riding round trying to figure out where the track goes and how much traction there is. I don't go hard, I just try and get into a rhythm and get a picture of the race track fixed in my mind. I've found that the European tracks have a different sort of surface to back home. European tyres don't seem to work back in America, but things feel different here. Perhaps it's the track temperature, or something. I never seem to have to worry too much about learning circuits, perhaps I learnt to do it quickly when I was an amateur back in the States. I used to have five different bikes to ride at the same race meeting, so I had to get the

The 'T' on Christian Sarron's 250cc Yamaha distinguishes it from his number one machine.

circuit sorted out really quick."

Alex Bedford, one of Britain's very few representatives in the 125cc class, was learning the Grand Prix circuits at the same time as Spencer. "One of the ways I learn a circuit is to go to a particular corner where I'm having problems and watch other people, the lines they take and how they match their gear changes to the braking." For someone like Alex direct instruction from an experienced rider can be a great help: "In Buenos Aires, Barry Sheene took me round for a few laps. He borrowed a road bike and I sat on the back. Before practice started I felt I already had an

Champion's Vince French discusses plug reading with Harald Bartol and Patrick Fernandez.

advantage over the others."

Lines and braking points are not always obvious: braking as late as possible may not be the fastest way round the circuit and Randy Mamola remembers a lesson he learnt from Steve Baker at Laguna Seca several years ago: "It was the first time I'd ridden a 750 at Laguna and I asked Baker if I could follow him. I found I could go into corners miles faster than he was but he was still getting round them quicker. He was braking early and then accelerating through the turn. I was braking so hard and late that I was getting all out of shape and couldn't get on the gas early. I tried doing what he was doing and immediately picked up two seconds which put me on the front row of the grid."

Fast pit work by the Yamaha team, trying to make the best use of limited practice time.

Most man-made race tracks have good enough visibility so that the exit of each corner can be seen before the rider is committed to the turn. It is simple for him, therefore, to choose his peeling off point, clipping the desired apex, accelerating steadily to use all the road on the exit. If the road undulates, half the corner may be obscured over the brow of a hill or, on a road circuit, it may be obscured by a bank or wall. When the exit of the corner is not visible the rider will almost certainly need to pick a marker to aim at for his apex. It may be a patch in the road, a certain kerbstone or even an object on the outside of the circuit that comes into view around the corner, just as he should be peeling off and heading for the inside.

Some riders find it important to sort out the gear with which they negotiate each corner at an early stage. This will depend on the individual's riding style. Riders who change down through the gears one by one, letting out the clutch each time, will always know which gear they are in and, more importantly, how engine speed is matched to road speed. But this method is hard on the transmission. It creates harsh torque reversals and may over rev the engine unnecessarily. Changing down through a number of gears without letting out the clutch until the gear changing is completed for the corner puts far less strain on the engine but the rider must be careful to count his gear changes or he can easily end up in the wrong gear for the corner. Too low a gear will cause the back wheel to lock up and slide, too high a gear will necessitate another gear change to bring the engine into the power band. The second method needs more practice as the rider must know that he needs to change down three gears for one corner, two for another and so on.

As the rider becomes familiar with the circuit, he will start to go faster and the gear he selects for each corner will change. Before he can hope to set his fastest possible lap time, however, he must choose the overall gearing that matches the performance of his engine to the circuit. Normally this is a simple case of choosing the final drive sprockets[2] that enable the engine to reach maximum rpm in top gear at the fastest point of the circuit. In special circumstances a rider may modify this if he feels that a slightly lower or slightly higher ratio will not lose him too much speed in a straight line but will give him perfect gearing for a certain corner.

Having exactly the right gear for a given corner can be a big advantage. If the rider can change down and find that the engine is

2   By choosing a different sprocket for the engine output shaft and/or for the rear wheel the relationship between the engine speed and the road speed can be varied. A smaller rear wheel sprocket or a larger engine sprocket means higher gearing which should give the machine a faster top speed. The opposite will make the bike accelerate quicker with a lower top speed.

Marco Lucchinelli practising on the NS500 Honda.

in precisely the right portion of the power band to give maximum drive through the corner, his speed onto the straight may be much higher. Finding himself between gears, where the lower choice has the engine screaming at the top of its power band with the engine developing so much power that the back tyre is spinning and sliding, or in too high a gear, so that the engine will not pull cleanly, will lose him valuable time.

Almost all the works Grand Prix machines now have alternative, internal ratios. Some machines have as many as four possible ratios, allowing the rider to choose the internal ratio that best suits the important corners on the circuit. Sorting out the internal ratios is a complicated task and most riders will draw a sketch of the circuit, making their gear changes and the gear that they think would be perfect for each corner. By doing this they can work out whether it is possible to build a gearbox that will exactly suit their needs. Even with 24 possibilities for the internal ratios and a larger number of overall ratios, circuits still often demand a compromise and a rider must always face the fact that sorting out his gearbox is only one of the many problems that he has to cope with in the limited practice time available.

There is no straightforward order for the machine's development during practice. One aspect of its performance affects another. The engine's carburation will have a great effect on the gearing both overall and for individual corners. Harald Bartol is one of the few, well-respected Grand Prix engineers who has had considerable experience as a rider. Firstly, he will set up the machine's carburation on his test bench but that alone is certainly not enough and track testing is very important. "With a new or modified engine I always like to run it on the test bench first, obviously to experiment with many things: ignition timing, exhaust pipes, disc valve timing and caburation. But in the end it is the engine's performance on the track which counts. The engine must be run in before we can get down to serious work. For track testing I will always start off with two or three sizes of main jet bigger than I was using on the test bench for safety. On a test bench the engine runs hotter and richer than it does on the track. Some tracks are better than others for testing. Misano is an example of a good track with a variety of corners and a reasonable straight. The Salzburgring is closest to my workshop but the engine spends too much time pulling up the hill and this confuses carburation. Now that I have retired from racing, I have no particular desire to ride and Patrick Fernandez has a very good feel for the engine. He can tell when it is too lean, whereas most riders only feel when it is too rich.

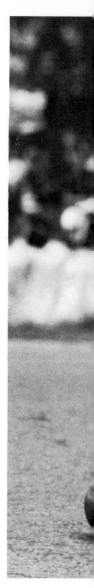

Kenny Roberts, pushing his tyres and machine to the limits.

"When an engine is lean, it revs very freely; when it feels that free it's best to check because you might be melting a piston. If it is much too lean, it will feel as though it is running out of petrol. When the engine is too rich, it will hesitate, almost like a misfire, or at least it will have a flat spot and not pull cleanly out of a corner. If the engine is very fast, always check preferably not only the spark plug but by looking at the piston. When the engine is running at its fastest it may be on the edge of failure."

Carburation is so critical because the engine produces the most power when it draws in exactly the right amount of oxygen to burn

the fuel, supplied by the carburettor, completely. Creating this power makes heat and complete combustion will generate so much heat that the piston melts. A little extra fuel is needed, therefore, to cool the piston. But too much fuel inhibits combustion, reducing the power output. This is true not only at full throttle opening, where maximum power is created, but also throughout the throttle range. Carburettors vary in their jetting systems but there are basically four things that affect the fuel mixture: the main jet, the

needle, the pilot jet and the carburettor slide cut-away. The pilot jet is situated on the engine side of the slide and comes into action as soon as air flows through the carburettor. Different carburettor slides have different cut-aways: a large cut-away makes the mixture lean, a small cut-away richens the mixture. Slide cut-aways and pilot jets greatly affect the way the machine starts and runs at small throttle openings, but the needle and the bore in which it runs, the needle jet, soon take over and control mid-range carburation. The

The talented Frenchman, Jean-Louis Tournadre, who always seemed to get his machines to perform superbly retired twelve months after winning the 1982 250 World Championship.

223

needle is tapered so that the hole it uncovers in the needle jet grows as the needle is drawn out. The size of the needle jet, the taper of the needle and the position of the needle in the carb slide all affect the mixture. At full throttle, the needle has been pulled out of the needle jet and the main jet size controls the fuel mixture.

Carburettors are complicated instruments and this is a simplified explanation of the jetting systems. Many racing carburettors now have a power jet which is a tube running from the float bowl to the mouth of the carburettor, through which the engine draws extra fuel as hard acceleration creates a depression in the mouth of the carburettor. The two stroke racing engine is critically affected by carburation and it is such a complex thing to get right a tremendous amount of time can be spent on it and it is virtually all trial and error.

Alain Chevallier is the first person to successfully break free of trial and error carburation. He has developed a system which uses a small computer to meter fuel to a second power jet which continually compensates for changes in atmospheric conditions and the engine's needs. To supply the computer with the correct information, Chevallier's system measures combustion chamber temperature, rpm and a third, secret, factor. Thanks to the sponsorship and involvement of Elf, the French fuel and oil company, Chevallier was able to use their electronics expertise to turn his ideas into reality.

When Chevallier goes testing he mounts a pen recorder[3] under a specially modified petrol tank and this monitors the values used by the computer. He uses this information to set the carburation to a realistic level by the conventional means of changing jets, etc. From then on the computer itself is left to make the fine adjustments and perfect carburation is ensured.

Fast lap times and winning races is not just down to learning the circuit and having a fast engine. Tyres are vital and tyre testing plays a very important part of development. Randy Mamola has done a lot of work with Dunlop in recent years and knows what tyre testing is all about. "Firstly, we get the bike sorted out on old tyres, get it handling reasonably well and carburating Okay. Then we put a first set of tyres on and of course with new tyres I soon pick up time. If I'm not using all the tyre on the front, then we'll put it on a wider rim and see what difference that makes. But we spend most of our time working with rear tyres. After I've tried one I come in and tell the tyre technicians what I think about the way it performs and they tell me how it's affected the lap time. What's important to

3   Paper is fed from a roll and one or more differently coloured pens scribe lines on the paper corresponding to varying levels in the factors under study.

do in testing is not to break lap records but to ride consistently. I normally ride at about 80% of my ability but I can hold it at that. When we think we've got a good set of tyres sorted out we normally end up doing about 20 laps more than race distance so that we can be sure that the tyres will last a Grand Prix."

Tyre development goes hand in hand with suspension because one affects the other. A tyre that provides more grip may well upset suspension and even the way a machine carburates coming out of corners will affect its handling and tyre performance. Suspension settings rely very largely on the rider's feel and different riders prefer different reactions from the machine. For example, Kenny Roberts seems to prefer hard suspension which means that he receives direct information about the tyres' contact with the road. Other riders opt for softer suspension that may result in the tyres maintaining better contact with the tarmac. Pinpointing suspension and handling problems can be a nightmare that relies a great deal on the rider's experience. A front end shake, or judder, may be caused by the wrong steering geometry or badly damped front forks, but it is equally likely to have been generated by a rear suspension problem or a twisting swinging arm. A machine that was handling perfectly one weekend may turn into a camel at the next circuit, forcing the rider and his team of mechanics to start all over again.

The easiest way for a rider to make progress with his suspension is for him to use two machines during practice. Anyone who can afford to, does so. It means that the rider can try one set of suspension settings or tyres, etc. then come in and use the second bike with a different set-up. A few seconds later he can be out on the track, making a direct comparison while the mechanics modify the first machine. After a few laps the rider will return to the pits to report on the reserve machine's performance, perhaps requesting some changes, and then waste no time in trying the first machine again.

Practice is not only for machine development, as practice times dictate the rider's position on the starting grid. In motor cycle racing it may not be so important if the rider is on the first or second row, but coming from the back of the grid may be a major disadvantage, especially if the path is blocked by other riders who are slow to start. More than anything a fast practice time, and preferably pole position on the grid is an important psychological advantage.

10

Race Day

Randy Mamola ready for battle with leathers and helmet, boots, gloves and knees taped ready for scraping across the tarmac.

The band started playing at six o'clock in the morning. Mechanics who had been working all night and riders who wished for more sleep did not appreciate waking so early, but at Assen, for the Dutch TT, where all six classes compete racing starts at 10am and the crowd has been there since midnight.

It is race day and all the preparation is finally put to the test. The rider should have but one aim: to arrive on the start line in the best physical and mental state to win. For some this is easy: they have no particular need for lengthy sleep the night before, they enjoy breakfast and even lunch. For others the night's sleep may have been interrupted by bouts of worrying and food is unattractive on race day. Their nerves become strained and tempers are short with those around them. Keith Huewen's experience is typical: "I think I sleep well, but my girlfriend says that I toss and turn terribly. I always think about the circuit the night before; there are two places where I think best. One is in the bath and in a race paddock there aren't any baths, and the other is in bed, just before I go to sleep. So I lie there and think about the circuit and the bike and I suppose I must carry on thinking about them when I go to sleep because sometimes I wake up knowing that I have to do something and then I have to get up and jot it down on a piece of paper so that I remember it the next day.

"One thing I really hate is to wake up early on a day when I don't race till late afternoon. I get terribly frustrated with the waiting and it's no good going for an afternoon nap just befor the race because I need at least an hour to wake myself up."

Most riders, like Martin Wimmer, need a quiet period of relaxation before they go out to race. "An hour before the race I go to my caravan and lie down. I close my eyes and ride around the track in my head. I work up my concentration and I know that it makes a lot of difference because I have experimented in practice, one time with lying down and concentrating and then without. It made the difference of one and a half seconds a lap. While I'm thinking about racing, my pulse rate goes up but about ten minutes before the start I get up, breathe deeply, calm myself down and go quietly to the start line."

Patrick Fernandez treats his race preparation differently. "I don't get too nervous on race day, perhaps because I have been brought up in racing. My father was Algerian Champion in 1952 on a Manx Norton and I first raced go karts when I was nine years old. I do like to have fifteen minutes before the race in the van, listening to music, making my brain empty and not thinking about racing. I don't make a plan about the race because no two races are the same and you must just be able to react to any circumstance."

The build-up to any Grand Prix is accomplished by a degree of razzmatazz, often with bands playing, occasionally an air display, almost always with a surfeit of girls carrying banners. It is easy to see that the riders are keen to shut themselves off from any distractions; even the most publicity conscious will only manage a mechanical wave to the crowd while he coolly thinks about the race ahead. Riders use the warm-up lap not just to get their tyres up to working temperature but also to get their minds working at racing speed, as Richard Schlachter explains: "As I set off on the warm-up lap, I weave the bike to and fro to warm up the tyres. I take it slow and easy for the first few corners, but speed up, working up my concentration. I talk to myself, telling myself to look further ahead, working at taking in that information, putting it in the memory bank. I think that's very important when you're racing: being able to think ahead while knowing where you are on the track, taking in the information about the road and using it at the right time without thinking about it. When I get back to the start line I keep up the concentration, telling myself to be aggressive. Even once the race has started I talk to myself saying 'Okay, you dummy, that's the second time you've peeled off too late for that corner, now let's do it right'. Every other rider on the start line is the man to beat. I think of them all as the enemy. During the race, sometimes I don't recognise individual riders, he is just a moving tree, an obstacle you have to find a way round."

Riders tend to be practical people and very few have superstitions but Barry Sheene always raced under the number '7' and constantly searched for associations with that number. He used pit number seven and if he could, stayed in a hotel room the numbers of which would add up to seven. He always wore a Gary Nixon tee-shirt under his leathers. Riders in general hate to wear new leathers or helmets for the first time in a race. Apart from the purely practical consideration that they may not fit properly, riders will hang onto their old and trusted garments as long as possible as new things are associated with bad luck.

On the grid the bikes and riders are beseiged by photographers. Roberto Gallina shades his team with an umbrella; Franco Uncini looks relaxed enough while his mechanics tend to a last minute detail.

Waiting to come under starter's orders for the 125cc Austrian Grand Prix in 1982.

The grid is often the scene of last minute panics: perhaps the
weather has turned sour and riders need to change from slick to
wet weather tyres, perhaps the engine has oiled a plug on the
warm-up lap or some other defect has been noted. Mechanics are
always on hand, often with a spare set of wheels ready to change
and always with a small toolbox carrying essentials for last minute
repairs: a spare set of plugs, locking wire and tape, pliers,

screwdrivers and spanners that might be needed for final adjustments. Some riders find it best to occupy their mind with the machine as the countdown continues to the start. They bounce on the seat, squeeze the front brake or compress the forks, testing the suspension. Although it is far too late to make any alterations it might help warm up the damping oil, but really it can have very little effect. For the tenth time the rider checks that the fuel has

The first corner, and all the development, practice and preparation are put to the test.

been turned on and that first gear has been selected. He might rock the machine backwards and forwards slightly, feeling the chain pull on the sprockets and the gears mesh loosely. But not too much or the engine will turn over, sucking fuel into the cylinder and drowning the sparkplug. The rider turns the handlebars from right to left as if to feel the machine's steering and checks that the steering damper is set correctly. He looks with concern at the engine temperature gauge. With the engine stopped, ready for the start, the water temperature does not show properly on the gauge. There is no water circulation because the pump is not running and the gauge shows a falsely high reading. If the engine temperature has got too high, the engine may not start. The same can happen if it has sunk too low.

With three minutes to go the mechanics were ordered off the grid and engines stopped. Things should proceed quickly to the start, but if the one minute and thirty second board are delayed riders may worry that the tyres are cooling down and extra caution will be needed at the beginning of the race. But once the thirty second board is shown there is little time to think of anything but fixing a gaze on the starter and his flag or lights. From that point it all comes down to the practised art and science of starting the bike and racing it for the full distance.

Everyone wants to know the winner and on the rostrum all the promotion girls try to get in on the act.

Randy Mamola soaks up the sun.

After any race there will be only one winner, with the rest as losers. Even winners do not always show immediate, ecstatic exuberance. The concentration and the adrenalin trip are a lonely experience that leaves the rider often temporarily unable to relate to the crowded congratulations heaped upon him. It is difficult to imagine, but Keith Huewen explains: "In a way it's the same whether I win or lose, it's an anti-climax. I'm numb to everyone around and I sign autographs automatically. I walk without thinking, just following the person in front of me. It's probably only when I go to bed that night that I think 'Hell, I enjoyed that race'. Then there are some races that I think about for a long time after and they're not necessarily the races that other people remember but those that I think I rode really well in. Perhaps it didn't come easy to me and I had to force myself to concentrate and think what I was doing."

Everyone loves a winner but often those who watch racing do not understand that every rider has had his own competition within the race. One may be bitterly disappointed at having finished second while another is justifiably well pleased at having finished fourteenth. A rider knows in his own mind whether he rode well or not, whether he raced better than the previous weekend and made the best of the machine or not. Some riders give excuses to their managers, mechanics and to the press but if they are to improve above all they have to be honest with themselves and sort out whether they could have gone faster or whether, on that day, in those circumstances, they did the best possible job.

Barry Sheene explores the maximum angle of lean.

11

After the Flag

Rob McElnea making use of the slab sided composite frame of the Skoal Bandit Suzuki.

With the race day over riders and mechanics alike turn their attention to the next circuit and the next event. Club racers will be returning to work on Monday to face five days of 'eight till five' until the weekend brings them to another race. The professional rider has only the next race to think about. Almost certainly the next circuit will be some distance away and during the Grand Prix year teams will travel some 20,000 miles following the world championship trail, and more to include the international races that they must contest in between.

The International meetings are vital to the privateers particularly because it is there that they earn the money that allows them to go GP racing. Unless he finishes regularly in the top ten at Grands Prix he cannot hope to win enough prize money to pay the running costs on his machine and the transport to the next meeting. The FIM and the GP organisers rely on the fact that riders want to go after world championship honours and never pay enough to keep the rider and machine out of debt. International events have to attract riders with reasonable start and prize money to get an impressive field that will attract spectators.

At a big International meeting a good privateer like Patrick Fernandez or Martin Wimmer might receive £1,000 or £2,000 in start money. A world champion can command £10,000 or more. So it makes sense for riders to fit in as many of these meetings as possible between GP commitments.

So as soon as the rider has crossed the finish line the team prepares to move on, unless there is something to celebrate when time will be found for the customary revelry. Often even parties must be cut short because in most cases GP paddocks open on Monday and there is a flat-out race across Europe to be set up in the best spots for the next week. Paddocks are rarely big enough for the huge transporters, caravans and motorhomes that now make up the 'circus'. Power points are usually limited and toilet facilities poor. Those who arrive late may not even get into the paddock and will certainly have trouble plugging into the power connections to

run lights and tools.

The FIM rarely seems to consult an atlas when deciding upon the Grand Prix dates and they follow no logical order. The next circuit is often 1,000 miles away and there may be two, three or more borders to cross. Border crossings are the most hated part of travelling for Grand Prix teams. Travelling from one country to another the racing bikes, spares, tyres and everything else in the transporter has to be exported, imported and then exported again.

The country the team is travelling through requires some assurance that the bikes, etc. are not going to be sold without any import duty being paid. To avoid leaving huge monetary bonds at every border each team carries a carnet which covers the contents of their transporters. The carnets are issued in the country where the team is based and act as a guarantee that, once imported, the goods will be exported again.

Life is seldom simple for the teams at border crossings. Customs officials may be over-worked, but more likely merely lazy, and it will often take many hours to go through the paper work required to process the vehicles and their contents. A wait of six or even twelve hours is not uncommon and occasionally the customs

Racing paddocks are crowded and it forces everybody to live together in a tight community.

No-one enjoys life more than Graeme Crosby.

officials will just decide that they cannot be bothered and will find some obscure reason not to let the team into the country at all. This happens most regularly when trying to get into Italy where the customs will not let anyone into the country with a machine unless they have had their entry accepted for the meeting they are intending to attend. It is no good trying to go to Italy and argue for a start when you get to the circuit. Very likely you will not even get into the country. There are no hard and fast rules about this though and most riders if refused entry at one border post will retrace their steps and try the next post along until they are allowed in. Perseverance usually pays off in the end but it can be another major source of aggravation that neither the rider nor the mechanic need.

Craig Ballington has his helmet tightened by Dad.

Some riders never get to like the travelling, changing money, different languages, cultures and foods. They may find the long periods away from home a strain. Kenny Roberts did not enjoy travelling and after six years in Europe he decided to spend the time at home and stopped racing in Grands Prix. "Things are so complicated now, the bikes, the tyres, and Yamaha always want me to do the testing, that I am spending just about all the year in Europe. It gets to you after a while, there always seems to be a new problem, someone wants an interview, or the bike is playing up. I'd do an awful lot better if I could get back home to the US for a while and relax."

Most riders enjoy the travel, etc. At least (at first) it has to be a tremendous change from the life they are used to, whatever country they come from and it is a challenge that is gladly taken up. The novelty eventually wears off and the travel to some becomes a bind and that is a contributory factor when the time comes to think of retiring from racing.

If one is considering what constitutes a successful racing motor cyclist then it makes sense to take into account the position in which he leaves the sport. Beyond enjoying the very sport itself and winning races the ideal would be to retire without permanent injury and with a reasonable standard of living to show for the years of effort.

The choice of the time to retire must be a very personal thing and there are many factors that affect a man's decision that enough is enough and he should race no more. If one asks professional riders they will usually say that their own performance is the deciding factor, as Richard Schlachter explains: "I will stop GP racing when I am no longer progressing. I think everyone knows when they get to the point when they are no longer improving, even then I might well go home to the States and ride a superbike or something

Riders and mechanics spend a good proportion of their time travelling, driving thousands of miles and making innumerable ferry crossings.

because I will probably still enjoy racing and I'll only finally stop when I don't enjoy it any more."

Some people retire from riding but keep close to the action by getting involved in the organisation. The two most successful men in this respect are Kel Carruthers and Roberto Gallina. Carruthers won the 250 World Championship in 1969 and since retiring has helped Kenny Roberts to win the 500cc world title in his capacity as team manager. Carruthers passed on his European Grand Prix experience to Roberts and this must be considered a major factor in Roberts winning the title at his first attempt. Roberto Gallina was not quite as successful as a rider but has shown himself to be Carruthers' equal as a team manager. Gallina has consistently had the most reliable Suzukis in the paddock and though he has had a variety of riders in his charge he has been able to help them all to attain a reasonably calm approach to their racing. Something rarely noted in the Italian temperament.

Both Carruthers and Gallina have been able to use their own hard-won experience to make life easier for riders in their charge and it is doubtful if anyone who has not raced themselves could converse with the rider on the same wavelength, telling him exactly what he wants to know and making sense of the information coming from the rider about tyres, engine, handling, etc.

The most successful rider of all time, Giacomo Agostini, took to car racing when he retired from bikes but eventually decided to return to two wheels and form his own team. He described the feeling he gets watching one of his riders like Graeme Crosby as 'frustrating', having never quite lost the urge to race himself. "I find being a team manager very satisfying but sometimes when Graeme comes in for a pit stop or just before the start of a race I have the urge to push him off the bike and have a go myself. When our team wins I get a great sense of achievement, but it is never quite like it was when I was riding myself."

Some riders claim that when they retire from racing they want to do something else entirely. Graeme Crosby may have given up Grand Prix racing but he did not find stopping riding altogether an easy thing to do and still needs it to finance his flying activities.

There are those who think little of retirement and cannot imagine anything being able to replace racing, and Graeme McGregor is one of them. "What else gives you the chance to do what you love doing and to set off any Monday morning to another country. Even if you don't like it when you get there you only have to stay for a few days and then you're off somewhere else . . .".

12

New Technology

Resin impregnated carbon fibre cloth bonded either side of a special Nomex paper honeycomb spacer makes just about the strongest structural material commercially available. It comes under the banner of 'composite materials' and bonded structures using combinations of Nomex or aluminium honeycomb and skins of fibre glass, carbon fibre, Kevlar or aluminium have such flexible and attractive properties that any serious motor cycle designer must consider their use. Such materials are being used increasingly for a variety of high performance vehicles from Formula One racing cars through boats and hovercraft, civil and military aircraft to the NASA Space Shuttle.

The era of the composite motor cycle is arriving fast and with the racing successes of the carbon fibre framed 350 Armstrong and the Skoal Bandit Heron Project 500 that Rob McElnea used with such effect in Grands Prix and home internationals there is every reason to think that more and more such machines will be seen on the race tracks of the world.

Development of moulding techniques is advancing fast and although the Armstrong and Heron frames are very much small production designs a mass production motor cycle suitable for road use will soon be possible and will surely follow racing success.

As always with new technology it is advancing on a broad front and only as experimenters gain more experience will it narrow to an obviously efficient line of development. The current machines, including the Armstrong, the Heron and Roberto Gallina's TGA 1, all use different construction materials and techniques with different advantages and disadvantages. They cannot all be right; perhaps none of them are.

To decide which material should be used for building motor cycle frames one must first look at the properties required. Lightness is a prime requirement because it has such an effect on performance, but of course it is lightness of the complete structure that is important so that strength for weight is the most important of the criteria because the frame must withstand severe stresses.

The prototype aluminium honeycomb Suzuki developed in co-operation with Ciba Geigy.

The prime function of the frame is to hold the engine in the correct position with respect to the front and rear suspension systems. There is very little scientific fact to enumerate on how stiff or strong a motor cycle frame should be and how much frame flex upsets handling. In general terms, though, the stiffer the frame the better it will handle and those who say that a certain amount of flex is necessary for 'feel' are mistaken. They should read such scientific papers as the 1978 SAE SP-428 on Motorcycle Dynamics and rider control if they are keen on wading through mathematical models, or reflect on the experience of the British Heron Suzuki team who have been able to compare rider response to mechanical loadings and deflection in a frame jig for Suzuki factory frames since 1979. The work was done recently as part of the background to the Heron Project 500 and was possible because they still have the old frames and the rider feedback from Randy Mamola and Graeme Crosby as well as Rob McElnea. The better the rider felt the frame handled the less distortion it allowed for a given load and hence they set about making an even stiffer frame.

One simple consideration should convince the doubter that flex is bad news: when a frame distorts it stores energy and there is no control over when that energy will be released, when the frame will uncoil and throw an unexpected load on the suspension, steering and tyres. The only place on the machine that such energy should be stored is in the suspension springs, where its release can be

The second version of the slab sided composite Suzuki was built in carbon fibre and raced for the first time in 1985 by Rob McElnea.

controlled and partially absorbed by the damping medium.

Forces will always take the line of least resistance so the suspension must be made compliant and the frame stiff. Now stiffness is not the same as strength. Strength is resistance to breaking and a very strong frame is one that will not break but it may still deform. A stiff frame will not deform but may fail completely; clearly a frame must be both.

One of the biggest mistakes that any designer can make is to consider the material without thinking about how he will use it, to use a new material in an old application, merely substituting new for old without considering all the properties of both materials. The article should be completely redesigned around the new substance. It sounds basic enough but it is amazing how many mistakes are made by people who should know better: remember the carbon fibre Honda wheel failure at Kyalami in March '84. This was a classic case of misuse of materials where the normal aluminium spokes were replicated in carbon fibre, making good use of the material's tensile strength but forgetting to accommodate the point loadings where the spokes were bolted to hub and rim. Aluminium and carbon fibre do not have the same properties; the very fact that two wheels were almost indistinguishable makes one suspicious about the design.

The same thinking should be applied to aluminium tubular frames: do they really make the best use of the material? It seems likely that the life of the tubular aluminium frame will be very short as better designs both for aluminium and other composite materials come into common usage. Aluminium tubes may have been fashionable at the time but when Harris Performance Products came to make Barry Sheene's Grand Prix frame for '84 they used steel. They had built aluminium frames but knew that they could make a steel frame that was no heavier than the works Suzuki aluminium frame yet stiffer. They have since developed their own twin spar aluminium frame.

One major problem is that many alloys that would offer good qualities of strength and stiffness cannot be welded without causing a loss of those properties or shortened fatigue life. Alloys may need heat treating after welding. In all, aluminium alloys can be difficult and expensive to use in tubular frames.

Aluminium can be used in different forms, as the original prototype Heron Project 500 demonstrated. This was carried out with the assistance of Ciba Geigy, who manufacture a whole range of composite materials and give invaluable advice on their use. Heron approached Ciba Geigy because of their experience through involvement in Formula One car racing as well as aerospace. All the top F1 cars are now made from carbon fibre and the bonded box construction makes excellent use of the materials.

Even within the family of composite materals there are several sub-sections. Heron chose to use pre-formed boards which encourage construction methods totally unlike any sheet aluminium monocoques, such as those used by Louise Christen for his LCR sidecars and solos and poles apart from the welding of tubular frames. The use of pre-formed boards has more to do with the cardboard cut-out models that you see on the back of a Cornflakes packet.

The materials are used in a peculiar manner because of their special properties. The boards are really two sheets of high tensile and compressive strength material separated by an ultra light filler that has the sole job of maintaining the distance between the two sheets. It is analogous to a steel 'I' beam but it is far better than that because the beam or sheet can be as wide as you like and the separator is evenly distributed across the surface. The perfect distribution of loads is one of the prime strengths of composite boards.

The use of the filler is immensely effective as it improves the section of the material and makes use of the facing material's

The 1985 NSR500 Honda threw out the under-slung petrol tank and reverted to a conventional position for the exhaust pipes and a twin spar frame.

strength in tension and uses that to resist bending loads. The improvement in stiffness should be considered of a pair of aluminium sheets bonded together, combined thickness 't'; the resulting piece has a weight factor 1 and a stiffness factor 1. If two similar sheets are bonded either side of an aluminium honeycomb also thickness t the result has a weight factor of only 1.03 but a stiffness of 7.4. Doubling the honeycomb thickness of 2t results in a relative stiffness of 39 and only 1.06 weight factor, a 3,800 per cent increase in stiffness for a weight gain of only 6 per cent.

The unseen filler is made either from Nomex paper or aluminium foil. Ordinary paper, glass fibre, foam or even wood may be used but not in high performance materials. The Nomex is the same material as used in the fire-proof car racing overalls and is a cloth rather than a paper, extremely strong when impregnated with resin.

The usual method of constructing the honeycomb is very similar whether it be aluminium or Nomex and starts with the material – unimpregnated Nomex paper or aluminium foil – laid out in sheets

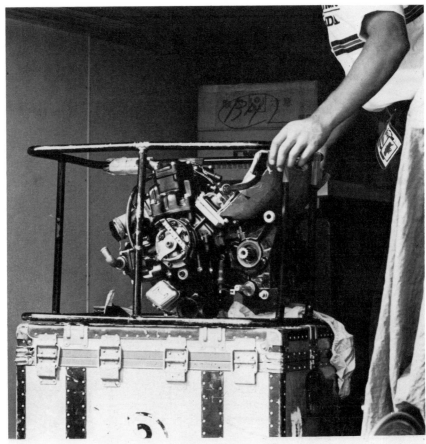

and then printed with lines of glue. The layers of material are built up one upon another and then compressed and cured. The resulting block of material is then cut into strips and the width of the strip will be the thickness of the finished filler.

Once the glue is cured the strips can be expanded from the top and bottom sheets. The result is that the block pulls into a honeycomb system with hexagonal cells. Two of the six sides are double skins glued together. The expanded Nomex has to be impregnated in resin and cured and then both are ready for use. Companies like Ciba Geigy make boards of composite materials and for this a sheet of bonding material is laid on either side of the expanded honeycomb, under the skin material.

Once cured under pressure the board of bonded composite is ready for a variety of uses and can be cut and bent to a useful variety of shapes. Bending the material requires that a section of the board that would form the inside of the curve be milled away. With a section of board removed the outer skin can bend and the honeycomb will collapse until the inner skins meet up and can be

Removed from the machine, the V-4 Honda engine looks a compact mass. The reed valve blocks can be seen behind the upward facing pair of cylinders.

253

bonded together; the join can be reinforced with a second strip of skin along the join. There are many ways of joining sections of board and of producing structural edgings. The Heron project bike uses structural filler, like a strong body putty to finish the edges of the frame. As an alternative, an aluminium machined or extruded section can be bonded along the edge. Similar filling with putty or better bonded in aluminium forms can be used to spread point loadings. In high stressed areas double skin thicknesses can be used but the board itself is so light that it may well be worth using a board that will withstand the greatest stress even if it leaves much of the structure over-designed.

Kenny Roberts on the works V four Yamaha in Spain.

Composite materials do not have to be used in board form though and the Armstrong carbon fibre frame is a first class example of a moulded frame. It makes use of the same sort of skin and filler system and gets the strength and stiffness for weight advantage for the pre-formed board system with the possibility of providing strengthened areas just where they are needed.

Manufacturing methods are completely different and start with pre-pregnated carbon fibre woven sheet. The pre-preg is a soaking of uncured resin that will eventually hold the orientation and position of the strands of carbon fibre. The fibres are carbon and make use of the fact that bonds between one atom of carbon and another are extremely strong. Carbon fibres have a carbon content of between 80 and 95 per cent and there are graphite fibres which are even stronger with a carbon content of 99 per cent.

Kevlar is a name that also crops up in composite structures and this a Du Pont brand name for a group called Aramid fibres; they are very different from carbon and graphite fibres but also draw their strength from the orientation of very strong intermolecular bonds. A Kevlar composite will not be as strong or as stiff as graphite but is less brittle. Carbon and graphite fibres will break at only 1 per cent elongation whereas Kevlar will stretch a little before failure. Kevlar is therefore more resistant to impacts and can be added to carbon fibres to form a hybrid that will not fail catastrophically when over stressed. This makes it a good material for use in helmets as a purely carbon fibre shell would disintegrate above a certain loading. It is less important for use in frames where extreme overloading will not occur unless the machine is crashed where the frame would have to be replaced even if the Kevlar was holding it together.

Probably the first Kevlar framed machine raced internationally was built by Steve Roberts in New Zealand. Roberts, a practical engineer who builds first class machines in his small back garden workshop, produced a monocoque Suzuki Formula One machine

which Dave Hiscock used in 1983. It replaced an aluminium monocoque prototype that had been built to test the frame layout and geometry.

Roberts also used the aluminium monocoque to make the mould from which three Kevlar machines were made. The suspension uses a single unit in tension mounted under the engine and the hand crafted swing arm and suspension are mounted on the back of the gearbox in an aluminium box sub frame. The monocoque runs from the top of the sub frame to the steering head taking the form and purpose of the fuel tank. Roberts used Kevlar in preference to carbon fibre for reasons of impact resistance.

The Armstrong CF frame does use some Kevlar content although the precise make up of the weave used is secret. To make certain that the cloth of fibres is completely impregnated with resin in the correct, controlled amount, the old-fashioned dry cloth and stippling with a brush dipped in resin that will do for small production-run fairings is not used for high performance mouldings.

The Armstrong frame is made using manufacturer impregnated cloth cut and laid up in a special mould. Each of the twin spars is made in a separate mould and that only produces a 'U' section. The mould is specially designed and then encased in a plastic bag that can be evacuated. Evacuating the bag sucks the cloth against the mould and then the bagged mould is placed in an autoclave oven. Such an oven can be pressurized so that the compression of the impregnated cloth into the mould is increased. The oven is heated to cure the resin.

Once set, the inside of the U shaped moulding is covered with a sheet of bonding film and then filled with a specially profiled honeycomb section and capped with another film of bonding material and pre-pregged cloth. The spar goes back into a vacuum bag and into the oven to cure the capping cloth layer and bond the whole thing together.

On the Armstrong, the two spars are joined at the steering head which has an insert of compressed fibre glass to take the localised loading of the steering head bearings. The swinging arm pivots and engine mounts are supported by similar inserts. The result is a very light and extremely strong structure and a similar method is used to make the swing arm.

There is no doubt that the method produces a very elegant product that is extremely strong and works very well. The one real drawback with the system is that modifications to the design are difficult and expensive, necessitating changes to moulds and bags. The pre-formed board system as used by Heron is much easier to

The carbon fibre Armstrong frame runs directly from the steering head of the swing arm pivot round the back of the gearbox. Barry Hart is seen here fuelling up the Armstrong fitted with his 500 3-cylinder engine.

alter even if the early frames did not look as well-finished as the Armstrong.

Roberto Gallina's TGA1 was the best looking machine of all and easier to modify than the Armstrong but less successful. The frame is made from three main sections: the steering head, which is fabricated from aluminium sheet, and the two spars which are machined from solid billets of aluminium. The concept of the twin spars is similar to the Armstrong and the aluminium is hollowed out into a similar 'U' section. That is filled with honeycomb and the section capped with a piece of sheet aluminium. The edges of the aluminium cap are bonded to the U section and reinforced by a strip of carbon fibre weave.

The TGA1 is machined on a numerically controlled milling machine. It requires an extremely high capital investment but alterations to the frame design are relatively simple and it is easy to produce several frames, enough for a team or even, say, 100 for sale.

One major attraction of using composites is that it does not require a high degree of technical knowledge or even skill. That does not mean that frame design is any more simple but at least the construction can be. The more that is done by the company like

Ciba Geigy the easier the frame is to make. Heron have gone furthest along this line by using the pre-formed boards and their method of construction requires no mould and very little in the way of a jig. The glueing can be done at room temperatures and paddock repairs are quite possible up to a point.

After an accident a tubular frame may well not reveal its damage to the naked eye and composite frames are similar. Complete failures will be obvious but it is possible for some carbon fibre, for example, to be broken without a total failure. The most reliable method of discovering such a partial failure is by using ultrasonics. A frame has an ultrasonic signature created by the way that the sound waves bounce around inside it. A fracture within the structure will cause a change in the ultrasonic signature. Few people will be carrying around ultrasonic testers in case they crash their composite frame but serious partial failures may be found by more simple methods. Hitting the frame with a screwdriver or a coin will perform a crude ultrasonic test and this should reveal if the skin has come unstuck from the honeycomb or if there are serious fibre fractures within the resin cloth composite.

There is more on the motor cycle that can be made out of composite materials than just the frame. Yamaha and Honda have already raced carbon fibre forks but these have not been entirely carbon but a core of steel tube wrapped in carbon cloth. Such tubes can be very strong and light and Ciba Geigy have supplied carbon fibre tubing for use in racing bicycles. The Gallina, Heron and Chevallier teams have all experimented with the carbon fibre discs that are much used in the Formula 1 car world. Chevallier has persevered and has employed a single cf disc which replaces two steel units, cutting total disc weight to a fifth. The disc used on the Project 500 is even more interesting because it is mounted on the rim instead of the hub and made by Lockheed.

The carbon discs are referred to as carbon carbon discs because there is no resin and the layers of carbon are held together because of the inter carbon bonds created when the disc is made under high compression and temperature. The disc pads are made from the same materials and disc wear is still a problem. Didier de Radigues retired from the '84 Swedish Grand Prix with his 8mm disc worn to a 3mm wafer and the remainder showing all the puff pastry edging signs that point to delamination thanks to overheating.

Composites can go a great deal further and it cannot be long before we see a large number of engine components made from carbon fibres or similar. There are still problems currently being solved and these include the orientation of carbon strands within a moulding. The orientation is very important as the strength of the article relies on the tensile and compressive strength of the fibres.

Con rods could benefit from the reinforcement of carbon fibres with technology as it stands now. It is easy to imagine how long strands of fibre could be bonded to the con rod, wrapped along the length of the rod and around the big and small ends.

The possibilities for using composite construction for advanced motor cycles are tremendous. With the right development they could even be cheaper than existing designs. A leading member of one design team has pointed out that this is possibly the reason why the Japanese have yet to become deeply involved in composite frame construction: they expect technological advances to be expensive.

New materials should encourage not only new frame designs but a rethink of suspension and steering systems. There are very few truly new designs but even those which have been tried and discarded before should never be totally ignored as in part or in total they may have something to contribute when new materials offer fresh possibilities.

So, what is new? You may ask. Jack Difazio built hub centre steering roadsters more than a decade ago and way back in the mists of time there was the Ner-a-car, with hub centre steering at the front of foot long swing arms which pivoted on the main chassis rails running the length of the machine and either side of the front wheel. That machine was first manufactured in Syracuse, New York, in 1921 and gained an enviable reputation for stability.

And yet the idea of hub centre steering has never really caught on. The Ner-a-car was last made in 1926 and although Difazio produced a number of complete machines production remained small scale. The same was true for others who ventured into the field, like the Quasar and Malcolm Newell's various admirable creations that have all missed out on mass acceptance and appeal. Only Difazio's have been raced, most notably on Mead and Tomkinson's Nessie endurance machine that attracted a great deal of interest but little international success.

The main thing missing from experimental steering and suspension programmes in the past has been the backing of a major manufacturer. That may be changing as several of the latest developments are supported by road bike manufacturers, including Honda, who have shown great interest in the latest Grand Prix Elf, and Bimota who have already shown both road and racing versions of their Tesi.

Once the ball starts rolling, and at the moment it is rather teetering on the edge, the motor cycle could be changed in many ways. Power assisted steering on a motor cycle may seem like a horrific idea but with the coming of hydraulically operated steering it cannot be far off and may be considered worthwhile on the large touring machines if not the racers of the future.

Although the touring machines have just as much to gain from an improvement over the current telescopic front forks it will be the sports and racing machines that attract the publicity and lead the way. The Bimota Tesi, for example, received a great deal of publicity even from the single race in which it competed during '84.

Unfortunately the development of the prototype 400cc roadster and 750cc racer cost so much that Bimota was bankrupted and only survived thanks to an Italian government plan allowing them to reschedule their debts.

Bimota were caught out by the need to rush through the project before the departure of the mastermind behind it, Massimo Tamburini. He was one of the founding fathers of Bimota and had endured enough of the high pressures of running that company, leaving to work with Roberto Gallina on the TGA 1 project.

What Tamburini left behind should probably take the prize for the most advanced motor cycle of '84, not only for the frame which was made from composite board like the Heron Project 500 but more particularly for the front steering system which is unique. It is a hub centre steering system operated by hydraulics.

The front wheel is suspended in a swinging arm that pivots just in front of the engine. The equivalent of the steering head bearings are inside the front wheel, in a bearing box about which the wheel rotates. The hydraulic piston acts between a small subframe mounted on the swinging arm and the bearing box. It is a double acting piston with hydraulic fluid on both sides so that it is pulled as well as pushed, a similar piston and cylinder is connected to the handlebars and two hydraulic lines run between.

It sounds complicated so why should anyone bother when the telescopic fork has managed to prop up the end of almost all motor cycles for the best part of fifty years? The answer is that while the telescopic fork may have been made to work very well this is more thanks to the amount of time and money heaped on its development than because it was a very good idea in the first place.

The telescopic fork has several features that makes the average engineer cringe at the very sight of them. Firstly they leave a large proportion of their length unsupported. If you look at any machine from the side you can see that all the loads are applied at the wheel spindle and lower fork leg, while the supporting triple clamps or yokes are at the other end. This means that *all* forks bend – if you have any doubts look at the fairings or radiators in a racing paddock. It will not be long before you find one that has been

Christian Leliard testing one of the 500cc Elf 2 prototypes with hub centre steering.

biffed by the front tyre, and that is not due to suspension failure.

It is not that this collision between tyre and machine causes the front wheel to lock, because I have not heard of that happening. The thing is that while the forks are bent under braking strain they are also supposed to slide up and down as the wheel encounters bumps. Bent tubes do not slide over each other freely.

Both fork legs bend the same amount if there is equal braking on each side of the wheel. On single disc arrangements this is not the case and one fork leg will bend much more than the other. Massive fork braces help but they are not the answer and you can often feel the forks twist and then unwind as brakes are applied and released.

Cornering forces also distort the forks thanks to the grip of the tyre which is acting towards the centre of the turn and the machine pushing in the opposite direction. This pushes the inside fork leg up and the outer leg down.

The forces that pass through the twisted forks are fed into the frame at the steering head, a woefully small area to absorb considerable loading. Many conventional twin loop tubular frames approximate to a triangle and with the usual steering head all the forces are put in at one apex. It would be so much better if they could be spread out or at least braced closer to reinforcement such as the engine.

The Tesi's hydraulic front steering may be very exciting and progressive but it is by no means the only avenue of approach. Every man and his dog has his own idea on what should replace the telescopic fork; the case against it is so simply explained that it is an obvious target and many possible replacements have merit.

Close to the Tesi system in engineering interest, and perhaps more likely to succeed thanks to the combined backing of Honda and Elf, is the Elf 2. Designed by André de Cortanze it included many of the features developed in his previous Elf endurance racers. The twin front swinging arms, both on the right hand side of the wheel, support a steering pillar at the forward end. The wheel spins on a stub axle built onto the pillar and it is the pillar that steers. There are no hydraulic actuators on the Elf as the pillar is connected to the handlebars by rods and linkages. On the prototype the handlebars did not pivot about a steering column at all but moved forwards and backwards on upright stalks, though for rider acceptance a dummy steering head was adopted in 1985.

The twin swing arms form a parallelogram, or at least a trapezium, so that the rake of the steering pillar and the trail it provides change very little as the suspension moves up and down. This is an advantage over the telescopic fork where rake and trail both change a great deal. Some loss of trail which provides for the

The space frame Hossack with its girder forks employing two swing arms and a suspension unit above the front wheel.

self-centering action is preferred, because although the trail may diminish, its effect increases as the weight of man and machine is heaped upon the contact patch under braking. The trick is to balance the change in geometry with the effect of weight and that is why there are trapeziums rather than parallelograms in the front suspension.

A similar system is to be found on the Tesi, for although there is only a single double sided swing arm, the steering bracket is anchored on both sides of the wheel to the frame. The connection is by very thin rods; they run through vertical slots in the front frame bulkhead and back to bearings above and behind the swing arm pivot.

The rods seem very slight but only have to work in tension because the braking forces provided by the Brembo callipers pull on the rods. Woe betide anyone who grabs the front brake while rolling the bike backwards. This is why the Tesi steering looks so complex; the triangle of tubes that makes up the steering subframe is bolted by its two foremost corners to the steering bracket. They form the forward upright of the trapezium, as does the steering bracket on the left hand side of the wheel where there are no hydraulics.

Between the two steering brackets runs this system's equivalent of the front wheel spindle. In the middle of the spindle is a short crossbar. On this crossbar are two bearings, one below and one above the spindle. These bearings replace the steering head races in the conventional frame and about them pivots a bearing box. On the outside of this box are the wheel bearings round which the front wheel spins. The hydraulic actuator runs between this bearing box and the rearmost apex on the tubular subframe. To the bearing box are bolted the calliper mounting plates.

The Tesi system is not that much more complex than most other steering designs; it just looks that way because most of it is hidden in the wheel instead of being spread outside. It is true hub centre steering whereas the Elf has its steering pivots within the wheel but outside the hub.

There are replacements for the telescopic fork that have their pivots outside the wheel, back up near the conventional steering head. The best known of these are built by Norman Hossack and Frenchman Claude Fior. Both are very similar, featuring a rigid girder front fork suspended on a parallelogram of short swing arms at the top front of the frame.

Viewed from above, these swing arms are triangular and the forward pointing apexes hold the spherical bearings about which the fork steers, substituting for the conventional steering head. The two swing arms pivot in the frame and although they spread the loads better than the old steering head they are still concentrated well away from the engine and swing arm, demanding a slightly larger and heavier frame than swing arm designs.

The Hossack and Fior systems do provide similar possibilities for the control of rake and trail as well as being stiffer than the telescopic fork. They may still bend under braking loads but are less likely to and have no sliding parts. They are better able to withstand differential forces on each leg. They look more like telescopic forks and are therefore easier to style for acceptance but the swing arms and steering linkages mean a high aerodynamic profile and centre of gravity. They do not suffer from the restrictive steering lock problems of the Elf and Tesi designs and the short swing arms can be light and stiff.

Yet another idea is a steering system that stands between the Elf 2 layout and the Hossack and these have been built by designers including Tony Foale, who also has his own version of the Hossack system, and Mark Walker who used it as his final year project for a mechanical engineering degree.

With a single one sided swing arm that runs towards the centre of the wheel to support the lower steering pivot bearing and an upper wishbone which holds the top bearing, this system offers some of

the advantages of both the designs it stands between.

Between the swing arm and the wishbone bearings runs a large section beam that holds the front wheel spindle at its lower end and a steering rod connection at the top. The swing arm and the wishbone form a trapezium but, considering the small angles through which the arms move, the steering angle, the trail and the machine's wheelbase alter very little – much less than a telescopic fork and very much better than the old leading and trailing link designs such as the old Greeves forks whose trail changed dramatically as the short swing arms moved through large angles.

The Foale style system employs a Lockheed peripheral disc. It gives a good deal more room in the hub for the bearings and both the Elf and the Tesi might also benefit. In fact the hubs could grow considerably, as long as the bearings did not become too heavy, and the wheels could be very much lighter as with rim mounted discs the spokes have little work to do.

Operating the steering is one thing but the telescopic fork also provided the suspension. Here the swing arm systems all gain thanks to the development of rocker arm rear suspension systems that provide any curve of rising spring and damper rate that the rider or designer might require. You can call them all rocker arm or linked systems, the Uni-Pro-Mono-Floater-Trak-Full-Link answer to the world's suspension problems.

Roberto Gallina built this TGA1 prototype in 1984, but it found little success.

The golden rules are simple for both front and back suspension. The system must not flex, for it is no good absorbing the input forces in the elasticity of the arms and linkages instead of the spring and damper because you will have no control over the time or violence with which the system uncoils.

The unsprung weight must be small compared to the sprung weight. The unsprung weight – wheels, tyres and part of the swing arm, linkages and shock – all move when they hit a bump and are separated by the sprung components – the rest of the shock and linkages as well as the frame engine and rider – which should not move when the bump is hit. Allow the unsprung weight to get too high and the spring would rather pass on the shock than absorb it and then all the unsprung weight begins to move.

The matching of springs and damper to the machine and use, as well as the exact linkage system employed, can only be arrived at after most of the machine is laid out but the heavy components such as the swing arms and suspension units should be mounted low. Both the Tesi and the Elf win out here over all other systems. The Elf had both units horizontal under the engine operating in extension rather than compression like the carbon fibre Armstrong , but after the prototype the units were moved to positions one each side of the engine and placed in compression because of the poor performance of the units in tension. The Tesi has both units vertical but low, in front of and behind the engine.

The telescopic fork is far from dead, though, as White Power are keen to demonstrate with their latest revival of the upside down fork. It is no new idea but they have the larger diameter external section of leg at the top. This means that a one piece unit can include fork yokes, and legs leaving much less unsupported overhang at the bottom. The lower internal sliders are only exposed for the length they need to travel. The disadvantage here is that fork braces to keep both sides going up and down together are not so practical. On the other hand the complete unit moulded mostly in a carbon fibre composite would be extremely strong and light, so it might keep the telescopic fork one jump ahead of the rest for little while longer.